HATHAYOGA PRADIPIKA

English Translation Accompanied by Sanskrit Text in Roman Transliteration

Swami Vishnuswaroop

Divine Yoga Institute
Kathmandu, Nepal

CONTENTS

INTRODUCTION

There are several fundamental texts in yogic literature on *Haṭha Yoga*. Among them *Haṭha Yoga Pradīpikā* by *Yogī Svātmārama* is a very popular one. Two other texts are *Gorakṣa Samhitā* and *Gheraṇḍa Samhitā* by *Yogī Gorakṣanātha* and the great sage *Gheraṇḍa* respectively. The fourth main text is known as *Haṭha Ratnāvali* which was written by *Srinivāsabhatta Mahāyogīndra*. It is considered that these texts have been written between the 6th and 15th centuries A. D. Another text known as *Śiva Samhita* which is considered to have been written/complied in 17th century A. D. All these texts explain the concept of yoga, its philosophy and practice so that one may attain the ultimate goal of human life – *mokṣa* or liberation.

The popular classical text *Haṭha Yoga Pradīpikā* has been translated into English and presented in its full form without editing/omitting any phrase or verse from the original Sanskrit text. It is seen that some of the authors/translators of *Haṭha Yoga Pradīpikā* and some classical texts on yoga and tantra have not included the original Sanskrit verses on *vajrolī*, *amarolī* and *sahajolī mudrās* in their books which are the practices of (tantric) sexual acts. They have considered that these *mudrās* fall in the category of 'impure *sādhanā* (practice)' and they are practiced by 'low-class *tantrics*'.

It was felt fair and necessary to include all the verses from the original text of *Haṭha Yoga Pradīpikā* on the *mudrās* and other practices and to translate them completely. Therefore, each of the Sanskrit verse of this popular text with its 'as it is' translation has been presented in this book. A sincere effort has been made in order to present the translation of this renowned classical text as simple and understandable as possible.

Haṭha Yoga is known as the science of purification. It is believed that total purification of all impurities on the physical level is absolutely necessary in order to purify the mind. When these impurities are eliminated from the body, the energy blocks are removed and *nāḍīs* (the subtle channels in the *pranic* body) function properly. Then the *prāṇa* moves freely throughout these subtle channels within the total physical structure.

Therefore, it is considered that various aspects of the practice of *Haṭha Yoga* e.g. *āsana*, *prāṇayāma*, *mudrā*, *bandha* and *ṣaṭkarma* serve as the solid foundation for the preparation and practice of *Rāja Yoga*, *Kuṇḍalinī Yoga*, *Kriyā Yoga* and *Tantra*. Originally, the science of *Haṭha Yoga* was not discovered for yoga therapy, but for the expansion and evolution of human consciousness. Although yoga has been scientifically proven to be effective in the treatment of many incurable diseases, the therapeutic effect of yoga is only a byproduct.

The objective of *Haṭha Yoga* is to create a harmonious balance between the physical body, *prāṇa* (the vital energy) and mind. It is said that when the impulses generated by this harmonious balance stimulate the awakening of the central force (*suṣumṇā nāḍī*), only then the evolution of consciousness is possible. The original objective of *Haṭha Yoga* is totally lost if it is not used for this purpose.

So much credit goes to my friend Mr. Jörg Moniz, France who wholeheartedly encouraged me and made valuable contribution for this work. I would also like to thank all my students I yoga participants from different parts of the world for their kind help and support in this work.

It should be noted that the original Sanskrit Text is in Devanagari along with its Roman transliteration. All the Sanskrit words I phrases that appear in the English translation are given in the transliterated Roman alphabets. For example, '*Svatmarama*' is written as '*Svātmārāma*' and '*Yogishvara*' as '*Yogīśvara*'.

It is hoped that the present text would be useful for all yoga students, yoga practitioners, yoga teachers and general readers who are interested in this subject.

Publisher

CHAPTER ONE

प्रथमोपदेशः

Discourse on Āsana

Salutation to Ādinātha Śiva

श्रीआदिनाथाय नमोऽस्तु तस्मै येनोपदिष्टा हठयोगविद्या ।
विभ्राजते प्रोन्नतराजयोगं आरोढुमिच्छोरधिरोहिणीव ॥१॥

śrīādināthāya namo'stu tasmai yenopadiṣṭā haṭhayogavidyā ।
vibhrājate pronnatarājayogaṃ āroḍhumicchodhirohiṇīva ॥1॥

Salutation to *Śrī Ādinātha* (the primeval Lord *Śiva*) who imparted the knowledge of *Haṭha Yoga* that shines forth as a stairway for those who desire to climb highly advanced *Rāja Yoga*. –1.

Salutation to Guru

प्रणम्य श्रीगुरुं नाथं स्वात्मारामेण योगिना ।
केवलं राजयोगाय हठविद्योपदिश्यते ॥२॥

praṇamya śrīgurum nātham svātmārāmeṇa yoginā ।
kevalaṃ rājayogāya haṭhavidyopadiśyate ॥2॥

Having saluted the Lord, his Guru, *Yogī Svātmārāma* imparts the knowledge of *Haṭha Yoga* solely for (achieving) *Rāja Yoga*. –2.

भ्रान्त्या बहुमतध्वान्ते राजयोगमजानताम् ।
हठप्रदीपिकां धत्ते स्वात्मारामः कृपाकरः ॥३॥

bhrāntyā bahumatadhvānte rājayogamajānatām ।
haṭhapradīpikāṃ dhatte svātmārāmaḥ kṛpākaraḥ ॥3॥

Rāja Yoga is not known due to darkness caused by various opinions and confusions. In order to dispel the darkness, the compassionate *Yogī Svātmārāma* throws light on *Haṭha Yoga*. –3.

First Haṭha Yogīs: Matsyendra and Gorakṣa

हठविद्यां हि मत्स्येन्द्रगोरक्षाद्या विजानते ।
स्वात्मारामोऽथवा योगी जानीते तत्प्रसादतः ॥४॥

haṭhavidyāṃ hi matsyendragorakṣhādyā vijānate ।
svātmārāmo'thavā yogī jānīte tatprasādataḥ ॥4॥

Yogīs like *Matsyendra*, *Gorakṣa*, etc. certainly knew *Haṭha Vidyā* (the knowledge). *Yogī Svātmārāma* knew it by their grace. –4.

Lineage of Mahāsiddhas

श्रीआदिनाथमत्स्येन्द्रशावरानन्दभैरवाः ।
चौरङ्गीमीनगोरक्षविरूपाक्षबिलेशयाः ॥५॥
मन्थानो भैरवो योगी सिद्धिर्बुद्धश्च कन्थडिः ।
कोरंटकः सुरानन्दः सिद्धपादश्च चर्पटिः ॥६॥
कानेरी पूज्यपादश्च नित्यनाथो निरञ्जनः ।
कपाली बिन्दुनाथश्च काकचण्डीश्वराह्वयः ॥७॥
अल्लामः प्रभुदेवश्च घोडा चोली च टिंटिणिः ।
भानुकी नारदेवश्च खण्डः कापालिकस्तथा ॥८॥
इत्यादयो महासिद्धा हठयोगप्रभावतः ।
खण्डयित्वा कालदण्डं ब्रह्माण्डे विचरन्ति ते ॥९॥

śrīādināthamatsyendraśāvarānandabhairavāḥ ।
caurangīmīnagorakṣavirūpākṣabileśayāḥ ॥5॥
manthāno bhairavo yogī siddharbuddhaśca kanthaḍiḥ ।
koranṭakaḥ surānandaḥ siddhapādaśca carpaṭiḥ ॥6॥
kānerī pūjyapādaśca nityanātho nirañjanaḥ ।
kapālī bindunāthaśca kākacaṇḍīśvarāhvayaḥ ॥7॥
allāmaḥ prabhudevaśca ghoḍācolī ca ṭinṭiṇiḥ ।

bhānukī nāradevaśca khaṇḍaḥ kāpālikastathā ॥8॥

ityādayo mahāsiddhā haṭhayogaprabhāvataḥ ।

khaṇḍayitvā kāladaṇḍaṃ brahmāṇḍe vicaranti te ॥9॥

Śrīādinātha (Lord *Śiva*), *Matsyendra, Śāvara, Ānandabhairava, Cauraṅgī, Mina, Gorakṣa, Virūpākṣa, Bileśayā, Manthān, Bhairava, Yogī Siddha, Buddha, Kanthaḍi, Koranṭaka, Surānanda, Siddhapāda, Carpaṭi, Kānerī, Pūjyapāda, Nityanātha, Nirañjana, Kapālī, Bindunātha, Kākacaṇḍīśvara, Allāma, Prabhudeva, Ghoḍācolī, Ṭiṇṭiṇi, Bhānukī, Naradeva, Khaṇḍa, Kāpālika* and many other *mahāsiddhas* (the great perfected yoga masters), having defeated death by the power of *Haṭha Yoga*, wander about the universe. –5-9.

अशेषतापतप्तानां समाश्रयमठो हठः ।

अशेषयोगयुक्तानामाधारकमठो हठः ॥१०॥

aśeṣatāpataptānāṃ samāśrayamaṭho haṭhaḥ ।

aśeṣayogayuktānāmādhārakamaṭho haṭhaḥ ॥10॥

For those burnt out by all types of *tāpa* (misery or pain), *Haṭha Yoga* is similar to a place of good shelter (that protects one from the heat). For those completely dedicated to the practice of yoga, *Haṭha Yoga* is the foundation like the tortoise supporting the world. –10.

हठविद्या परं गोप्या योगिना सिद्धिमिच्छता ।

भवेद्वीर्यवती गुप्ता निर्वीर्या तु प्रकाशिता ॥११॥

haṭhavidyā paraṃ gopyā yoginā siddhimicchatā ।

bhavedvīryavatī guptā nirvīryā tu prakāśitā ॥11॥

A yogī desirous of achieving success should keep the knowledge of *Haṭha Yoga* very secret for it becomes powerful if it is kept secret, and it becomes weak when (carelessly) revealed. –11.

Place of Practice

सुराज्ये धार्मिके देशे सुभिक्षे निरुपद्रवे ।

धनुः प्रमाणपर्यन्तं शिलाग्निजलवर्जिते ।

एकान्ते मठिकामध्ये स्थातव्यं हठयोगिना ॥१२॥

surājye dhārmike deśe subhikṣe nirupadrave ।

dhanuḥ pramāṇaparyantaṃ śilāgnijalavarjite ।

ekānte maṭhikāmadhye sthātavyaṃ haṭhayoginā ॥12॥

The *Haṭha Yoga* practitioner should live alone in a *maṭhikā* (a small shelter or hermitage of a yogī) in a solitary place free from rocks, water and fire to the extent of a bow's length, and in a well-ruled religious country without any disturbances where enough food can be obtained in alms. –12.

अल्पद्वारमरन्ध्रगर्तविवरं नात्युच्चनीचायतं

सम्यग्गोमयसान्द्रलिप्तममलं निःशेसजन्तूज्झितम् ।

बाह्ये मण्डपवेदिकूपरुचिरं प्राकारसंवेष्टितं

प्रोक्तं योगमठस्य लक्षणमिदं सिद्धैर्हठाभ्यासिभिः ॥१३॥

alpadvāramarandhragartavivaraṃ nātyuccanīcāyataṃ

samyaggomayasāndraliptamamalaṃ niḥśesajantūjjhitam ।

bāhye maṇḍapavedikūparuciraṃ prākārasaṃveṣṭitaṃ

proktaṃ yogamaṭhasya lakṣaṇamidāṃ siddhairhaṭhābhyāsibhiḥ । 13 ।

The *yoga maṭha* (shelter or hermitage of a yogī) should have a small door without any windows and be free from holes and hollows. It should be neither too high nor too low. It should be well smeared over with cow dung, be perfectly clean, and should be free from all kinds of insects or animals. Outside it there should be a pleasant *maṇḍapa* (an open platform), a *vedi* (a sacrificial alter or ground) and a well. It should be surrounded by a wall. These characteristics of a *yoga maṭha* have been described by the *siddhas* (perfected masters) of *Haṭha Yoga*. –13.

एवं विधे मठे स्थित्वा सर्वचिन्ताविवर्जितः ।

गुरूपदिष्टमार्गेण योगमेव समभ्यसेत् ॥१४॥

evaṃvidhe maṭhe sthitvā sarvacintāvivarjitaḥ ।

gurūpadiṣṭamārgeṇa yogameva samabhyaset ॥14॥

In this way, the yogī living in a yoga shelter (as described above), being free from all anxieties should practice yoga properly as instructed or taught by his guru. –14.

Causes of Failure and Success in Yoga Sādhanā

अत्याहारः प्रयासश्च प्रजल्पो नियमाग्रहः ।

जनसङ्गश्च लौल्यं च षड्भिर्योगो विनश्यति ॥१५॥

atyāhāraḥ prayāsaśca prājalpo niyamāgrahaḥ ।

janasaṅgaśca laulyaṃ ca ṣaḍbhiryogo vinaśyati ॥15॥

Yoga is destroyed by these six causes: over-eating, over-exertion, talkativeness, adherence to (conventional) rules, company of common people and unsteadiness. –15.

उत्साहात्साहसाद्धैर्यात्तत्त्वज्ञानाश्च निश्चयात् ।

जनसङ्गपरित्यागात्षड्भिर्योगः प्रसिद्ध्यति ॥१६॥

utsāhātsāhasāddhairyāttattvajñānāśca niścayāt ।

janasaṅgaparityāgātṣaḍbhiryogaḥ prasiddhyati ॥16॥

The following six bring success in yoga: enthusiasm, courage, perseverance, knowledge of the truth, faith and giving up the company of common people. –16.

Description of Yama and Niyama

अथ यमनियमाः ।

अहिंसा सत्यमस्तेयं ब्रह्मचर्यं क्षमा धृतिः ।

दयार्जवं मिताहारः शौचं चैव यमा दश ॥१७॥

atha yamaniyamāḥ ।

Now *yama* and *niyama* are described.

ahiṃsā satyamasteyaṃ brahmacaryaṃ kṣamā dhṛtiḥ ।

dayārjavaṃ mitāhāraḥ śaucaṃ caiva yamā daśa ॥17॥

Non-violence, truth, non-stealing, continence, forgiveness, endurance, compassion, humility, moderate diet and purity – these ten constitute *yama* (the rules of conduct). –17.

तपः सन्तोष आस्तिक्यं दानमीश्वरपूजनम् ।

सिद्धान्तवाक्यश्रवणं ह्रीमती च तपो हुतम् ।

नियमा दश सम्प्रोक्ता योगशास्त्रविशारदैः ॥१८॥

tapaḥ santoṣa āstikyaṃ dānamīśvarapūjanam ।

siddhāntavākyaśravaṇaṃ hrīmatī ca tapo hutam ।

niyamā daśa samproktā yogaśāstraviśāradaiḥ ॥18॥

The ten *niyamas* (the rules of self-control) are: austerity, contentment, belief in God, charity, worship of God, hearing the discourse of sacred doctrines (on Ultimate Truth), modesty, right thought, observance of vows and sacrifice. These ten *niyamas* are told by those experts in yoga. –18.

Description of Āsana

अथ आसनम् ।

हठस्य प्रथमाङ्गत्वादासनं पूर्वमुच्यते ।

कुर्यात्तदासनं स्थैर्यमारोग्यं चाङ्गलाघवम् ॥१९॥

atha āsanam ।

Now āsana is described.

haṭhasya prathamāṅgatvādāsanaṃ pūrvamucyate ।

kuryāttadāsanaṃ sthairyamārogyaṃ cāṅgalāghavam ॥19॥

Āsana is described first, because it is the beginning part of *Haṭha Yoga*. It should be practiced for gaining steadiness (of the body and mind), good health and lightness of physical limbs. -19.

वशिष्ठाद्यैश्च मुनिभिर्मत्स्येन्द्राद्यैश्च योगिभिः ।

अङ्गीकृतान्यासनानि कथ्यन्ते कानिचिन्मया ॥२०॥

vaśiṣṭhādyaiśca munibhirmatsyendrādyaiśca yogibhiḥ ।

aṅgīkṛtānyāsanāni kathyante kānicinmayā ॥20॥

I am going to describe some of the āsanas accepted by those enlightened sages like *Vaśiṣṭha*, and yogīs like *Matsyendra*. –20.

Svastikāsana (Auspicious Pose)

जानूर्वोरन्तरे सम्यक्कृत्वा पादतले उभे ।

ऋजुकायः समासीनः स्वस्तिकं तत्प्रचक्षते ॥२१॥

jānūrvorantare samyakkṛtvā pādatale ubhe ।

ṛjukāyaḥ samāsīnaḥ svastikaṃ tatpracakṣate ॥21॥

Having properly inserted both soles of the feet between the thighs and calves of the legs, sit perfectly balanced with the body upright. This is called *svastika* (*āsana*). –21.

Gomukhāsana (Cow's Face Pose)

सव्ये दक्षिणगुल्कं तु पृष्ठपार्श्वे नियोजयेत् ।

दक्षिणेऽपि तथा सव्यं गोमुखं गोमुखाकृतिः ॥२२॥

savye dakṣiṇagulpha tu pṛṣṭhapārśve niyojayet ।

dakṣiṇe'pi tathā savyaṃ gomukhaṃ gomukhākṛtiḥ ॥22॥

Place the right ankle next to the left buttock and the left ankle next to the right buttock. This is called *gomukha* (*āsana*) and it looks like the face of a cow. –22.

Virāsana (Hero's Pose)

एकं पादं तथैकस्मिन्विन्यसेदुरुणि स्थिरम् ।

इतरस्मिंस्तथा चोरुं वीरासनमितीरितम् ॥२३॥

ekaṃ pādaṃ tathaikasminvinyasedūruṇi sthiram ।

itarasminstathā coruṃ vīrāsanamitīritam ॥23॥

Place one foot on the side of the opposite thigh and the other foot under the same thigh. This is called *vīrāsana*. –23.

Kurmāsana (Tortoise Pose)

गुदं निरुध्य गुल्फाभ्यां व्युत्क्रमेण समाहितः ।

कूर्मासनं भवेदेतदिति योगविदो विदुः ॥२४॥

gudaṃ nirudhya gulphābhyāṃ vyutkrameṇa samāhitaḥ ।

kūrmāsanaṃ bhavedetaditi yogavido viduḥ ॥24॥

Press the anus firmly with the ankles, keeping them in opposite direction from one another, and sit calmly. This is known as *kūrmāsana* (tortoise pose) according to the yoga experts. –24.

Kukkutāsana (Cockerel Pose)

पद्मासनं तु संस्थाप्य जानूर्वोरन्तरे करौ ।

निवेश्य भूमौ संस्थाप्य व्योमस्थं कुक्कुटासनम् ॥२५॥

padmāsanaṃ tu saṃsthāpya jānūrvorantare karau ।

niveśya bhūmau saṃsthāpya vyomasthaṃ kukkuṭāsanam ॥25॥

Sitting in the *padmāsana* (lotus pose) insert the hands between the thighs and calves. Place the hands firmly on the ground and raise the body in the air. This is *kukkutāsana*. –25.

Uttāna Kurmāsana (Stretching Tortoise Pose)

कुक्कुटासनबन्धस्थो दोर्भ्यां सम्बद्य कन्धराम् ।

भवेद्कूर्मवदुत्तान एतदुत्तानकूर्मकम् ॥२६॥

kukkuṭāsanabandhastho dorbhyāṃ sambadhya kandharām ।

bhavetkūrmavaduttāna etaduttānakūrmakam ॥26॥

Sitting in the *kukkutāsana*, place your lower arms (hands) together with the neck and lie down flat like a tortoise. This is called *uttāna kūrmaka* (*āsana*). –26.

Dhanurāsana (Bow Pose)

पादाङ्गुष्ठौ तु पाणिभ्यां गृहीत्वा श्रवणावधि ।

धनुराकर्षणं कुर्याद्धनुर्आसनमुच्यते ॥२७॥

pādāṅguṣṭhau tu pāṇibhyāṃ gṛhītvā śravaṇāvadhi ।

dhanurākarṣaṇaṃ kuryāddhanurāsanamucyate ॥27॥

Grabbing the toes with the hands, pull them up towards the ears just like drawing a bow. This is called *dhanurāsana*. –27.

Matsyedrāsana (Spinal Twist Pose)

वामोरुमूलार्पितदक्षपादं जानोर्बहिर्वेष्टितवामपादम् ।

प्रगृह्य तिष्ठेत्परिवर्तिताङ्गः श्रीमत्स्यनाथोदितमासनं स्यात् ॥२८॥

vāmorumūlārpitadakṣapādaṃ

jānorbahirveṣṭitavāmapādam ।

pragṛhya tiṣṭhetparivartitāṅgaḥ

śrīmatsyanāthoditamāsanaṃ syāt ॥28॥

Place the right foot at the bottom of the left thigh and the left foot at the side of the right knee. Take hold of the left foot with the right hand, pass the left arm behind the waist and turn your torso and head towards the left. This is the *āsana* spoken of by Śrī *Matsyendranātha*. –28.

मत्स्येन्द्रपीठं जठरप्रदीप्तिं प्रचण्डरुग्मण्डलखण्डनास्त्रम् ।

अभ्यासतः कुण्डलिनीप्रबोधं चन्द्रस्थिरत्वं च ददाति पुंसाम् ॥२९॥

matsyendrapīṭhaṃ jaṭharapradīptiṃ

pracaṇḍarugmaṇḍalakhaṇḍanāstram ।

abhyāsataḥ kuṇḍalinīprabodhaṃ

candrasthiratvaṃ ca dadāti puṃsām ॥29॥

Matsyendrāsana increases the digestive fire. It is a weapon to destroy the multifarious terrible diseases in the body. *Kuṇḍalinī* is aroused through its practice and it stabilizes the moon (seminal fluid) of the wise practitioner. –29.

Paścimottānāsana (Back Stretching Pose)

प्रसार्य पादौ भुवि दण्डरूपौ दोर्भ्यां पदाग्रद्वितयं गृहीत्वा ।

जानूपरिन्यस्तललाटदेशो वसेदिदं पश्चिमतानमाहुः ॥३०॥

prasārya pādau bhuvi daṇḍarūpau

dorbhyāṃ padāgradvitayaṃ gṛhītvā ।

jānūparinyastalalāṭadeśo

vasedidāṃ paścimatānamāhuḥ ॥30॥

Stretch out both legs like sticks on the ground, and holding the toes of the feet with the hands, sit with the forehead placed on the knees. This is called *paścimotāna* (*āsana*). –30.

इति पश्चिमतानमासनाग्र्यं पवनं पश्चिमवाहिनं करोति ।

उदयं जठरानलस्य कुर्याद् उदरे कार्श्यमरोगतां च पुंसाम् ॥३१॥

iti paścimatānamāsanāgryaṃ

pavanaṃ paścimavāhinaṃ karoti ।

udayaṃ jaṭharānalasya kuryādudare

kārśyamarogatāṃ ca puṃsām ॥31॥

This *paścimotānāsana* is the most excellent of all *āsanas*. It makes the *pavana* (literally, air which means vital energy) flow through *suṣumnā*, stimulates the digestive fire, makes the belly lean and removes all the diseases of the practitioner. –31.

Mayūrāsana (Peacock Pose)

धरामवष्टभ्य करद्वयेन तत्कूर्परस्थापितनाभिपार्श्वः ।

उच्चासनो दण्डवदुत्थितः खे मायूरमेतत्प्रवदन्ति पीठम् ॥३२॥

dharāmavaṣṭabhya karadvayena

tatkūrparasthāpitanābhipārśvaḥ ।

uccāsano daṇḍavadutthitaḥ khe

syānmāyūrametatpravadanti pīṭham ॥32॥

Supporting the body on top of both hands on the ground, place the elbows at the sides of the navel. Raise the body in a higher position like a stick in the air. This is called *mayūrāsana* (by the experts of yoga). –32.

हरति सकलरोगानाशु गुल्मोदरादीन्

अभिभवति च दोषानासनं श्रीमयूरम् ।

बहु कदशनभुक्तं भस्म कुर्यादशेषं

जनयति जठराग्निं जारयेत्कालकूटम् ॥३३॥

harati sakalarogānāśu gulmodarādīn

abhibhavati ca doṣānāsanaṃ śrīmayūram ।

bahu kadaśanabhuktaṃ bhasma kuryādaśeṣaṃ

janayati jaṭharāgni jārayetkālakūṭam ॥33॥

This *āsana* destroys all diseases of the glands and spleen, and various disorders of the stomach. It removes the imbalances of the bodily humors (wind, bile or phlegm). It turns into ashes all the food eaten in excess, stimulates the digestive fire and even destroys the effect of *kālakuta* (a deadly poison). –33.

Śavāsana (Corpse Pose)

उत्तानं शबवद्भूमौ शयनं तच्छवासनम् ।

शवासनं श्रान्तिहरं चित्तविश्रान्तिकारकम् ॥३४॥

uttānaṃ śabavadbhūmau śayanaṃ tacchavāsanam ।

śavāsanaṃ śrāntiharaṃ cittaviśrāntikārakam ॥34॥

Lie flat on the ground on your back with your face upwards, like a dead man. This is called *śavāsana*. It removes tiredness and makes the mind calm. –34.

चतुरशीत्यासनानि शिवेन कथितानि च ।

तेभ्यश्चतुष्कमादाय सारभूतं ब्रवीम्यहम् ॥३५॥

caturaśītyāsanāni śivena kathitāni ca ।

tebhyaścatuṣkamādāya sārabhūtaṃ bravīmyaham ॥35॥

There are eighty-four *āsanas* as told by Lord *Śiva*. Out of those, I will describe the four most essential ones now. –35.

सिद्धं पद्मं तथा सिंहं भद्रं वेति चतुष्टयम् ।

श्रेष्ठं तत्रापि च सुखे तिष्ठेत्सिद्धासने सदा ॥३६॥

siddhaṃ padmaṃ tathā siṃhaṃ bhadraṃ ceti catuṣṭayam ।

śreṣṭhaṃ tatrāpi ca sukhe tiṣṭhetsiddhāsane sadā ॥36॥

Those four *āsanas* are: *siddhāsana, padmāsana, simhāsana* and *bhadrāsana*. However, *siddhāsana* is the most excellent of all (these *āsanas*). One should always sit with comfort in this pose. –36.

Siddhāsana (Adept's Pose)

अथ सिद्धासनम् ।

योनिस्थानकमङ्घ्रिमूलघटितं कृत्वा दृढं विन्यसेत्

मेण्ढ्रे पादमथैकमेव हृदये कृत्वा हनुं सुस्थिरम् ।

स्थाणुः संयमितेन्द्रियोऽचलदृशा पश्येद्भ्रुवोरन्तरं

ह्येतन्मोक्षकपाटभेदजनकं सिद्धासनं प्रोच्यते ॥३७॥

atha siddhāsanam ।

Now *siddhāsana* is described.

yonisthānakamaṅghrimūlaghaṭitaṃ kṛtvā dṛḍhaṃ vinyaset

meḍhre pādamathaikameva hṛdaye kṛtvā hanuṃ susthiram ।

sthāṇuḥ saṃyamitendriyo'caladṛśā paśyedbhruvorantaraṃ

hyetanmokṣakapāṭabhedajanakaṃ siddhāsanaṃ procyate ॥37॥

Press the perineum firmly with one heel and place the other heel above the genitals. Fix the chin properly on the chest. Remain firm, with senses under control, and gaze steadily at the eyebrow center. It is called *siddhāsana* and it breaks open the door to *mokṣa* (liberation). –37.

मेण्ढ्रादुपरि विन्यस्य सव्यं गुल्फं तथोपरि ।

गुल्फान्तरं च निक्षिप्य सिद्धासनमिदं भवेत् ॥३८॥

meḍhrādupari vinyasya savyaṃ gulphaṃ tathopari ।

gulphāntaraṃ ca nikṣipya siddhāsanamidāṃ bhavet ॥38॥

Place the right heel above the penis and the left on top of it (the right). This *siddhāsana* is performed also by inserting the heel in between. –38.

एतत्सिद्धासनं प्राहुरन्ये वज्रासनं विदुः ।

मुक्तासनं वदन्त्येके प्राहुर्गुप्तासनं परे ॥३९॥

etatsiddhāsanaṃ prāhuranye vajrāsanaṃ viduḥ ।

muktāsanaṃ vadantyeke prāhurguptāsanaṃ pare ॥39॥

This is called *siddhāsana*. Others know it as *vajrāsana*, some call it *muktāsana* and still others know it as *guptāsana*. –39.

Importance of Siddhāsana

यमेष्विव मिताहारमहिंसा नियमेष्विव ।

मुख्यं सर्वासनेष्वेकं सिद्धाः सिद्धासनं विदुः ॥४०॥

yameṣviva mitāhāramahiṃsā niyameṣviva ।

mukhyaṃ sarvāsaneṣvekaṃ siddhāḥ siddhāsanaṃ viduḥ ॥40॥

As among *yamas*, a moderate diet is the most important and among *niyams*, non-violence, so the *siddhas* consider that *siddhāsana* is the most important of all the *āsanas*. –40.

चतुरशीतिपीठेषु सिद्धमेव सदाभ्यसेत् ।

द्वासप्ततिसहस्राणां नाडीनां मलशोधनम् ॥४१॥

caturaśītipīṭheṣu siddhameva sadābhyaset ।

dvāsaptatisahasrāṇāṃ nāḍīnāṃ malaśodhanam ॥41॥

Of all the eighty-four *āsanas*, one should always practice *siddhāsana*. It purifies the impurities of seventy-two thousand *nāḍīs*. –41.

आत्मध्यायी मिताहारी यावद्द्वादशवत्सरम् ।

सदा सिद्धासनाभ्यासाद्योगी निष्पत्तिमाप्नुयात् ॥४२॥

ātmadhyāyī mitāhārī yāvaddvādaśavatsaram ।

sadā siddhāsanābhyāsādyogī niṣpattimāpnuyāt ॥42॥

The yogī who meditates on his *Aātmā* (the Self), takes a moderate diet and constantly practices *siddhāsana* for twelve years, attains perfection. –42.

किमन्यैर्बहुभिः पीठैः सिद्धे सिद्धासने सति ।

प्राणानिले सावधाने बद्धे केवलकुम्भके ।

उत्पद्यते निरायासात्स्वयमेवोन्मनी कला ॥४३॥

kimanyairbahubhiḥ pīṭhaiḥ siddhe siddhāsane sati ।

prāṇānile sāvadhāne baddhe kevalakumbhake ।

utpadyate nirāyāsātsvayamevonmanī kalā ॥43॥

When perfection is attained through the practice of *siddhāsana*, what is the use of practicing various other *āsanas*? When the *prāṇa* is made stable by the practice of *kevala kumbhaka*, *unmanī* (a mindless state) arises by itself without any effort. –43.

तथैकास्मिन्नेव दृढे सिद्धे सिद्धासने सति ।

बन्धत्रयमनायासात्स्वयमेवोपजायते ॥४४॥

tathaikāsminneva dṛḍhe siddhe siddhāsane sati ।

bandhatrayamanāyāsātsvayamevopajāyate ॥44॥

Thus, by firmly securing perfection in *siddhāsana* alone, the three *bandhas* occur by themselves without any effort. –44.

नासनं सिद्धसदृशं न कुम्भः केवलोपमः ।

न खेचरीसमा मुद्रा न नादसदृशो लयः ॥४५॥

nāsanaṃ siddhasadṛśaṃ na kumbhaḥ kevalopamaḥ ।

na khecarī samā mudrā na nādasadṛśo layaḥ ॥45॥

There is no *āsana* similar to *siddhāsana*, no *kumbhaka* similar to *kevala* (spontaneous retention of breath), no *mudrā* like *khecarī* and no *laya* (absorption of mind) like *nāda* (the inner mystical sound). –45.

Padmāsana (Lotus Pose)

अथ पद्मासनम् ।

वामोरूपरि दक्षिणं च चरणं संस्थाप्य वामं तथा

दक्षोरूपरि पश्चिमेन विधिना धृत्वा कराभ्यां दृढम् ।

अङ्गुष्ठौ हृदये निधाय चिबुकं नासाग्रमालोकयेत्

एतद्व्याधिविनाशकारि यमिनां पद्मासनं प्रोच्यते ॥४६॥

atha padmāsanam ।

Now *padmāsana* is described.

vāmorūpari dakṣiṇaṃ ca caraṇaṃ saṃsthāpya vāmaṃ tathā

dakṣorūpari paścimena vidhinā dhṛtvā karābhyāṃ dṛḍham ।

aṅguṣṭhau hṛdaye nidhāya cibukaṃ nāsāgramālokayet

etadvyādhivināśakāri yamināṃ padmāsanaṃ procyate ॥46॥

Place the right foot (at the root of) the left thigh and the left foot (at the root of) the right thigh. Cross the hands behind the back and firmly take hold of the toes. Place the chin firmly on the chest and gaze at the tip of the nose. This is called *padmāsana*, the destroyer of the diseases of the *yamis* (observers of *yamas*). –46.

उत्तानौ चरणौ कृत्वा ऊरुसंस्थौ प्रयत्नतः ।

ऊरुमध्ये तथोत्तानौ पाणी कृत्वा ततो दृशौ ॥४७॥

uttānau caraṇau kṛtvā ūrusaṃsthau prayatnataḥ ।

ūrumadhye tathottānau pāṇī kṛtvā tato dṛśau ॥47॥

Place the feet on the thighs with the soles turned upward and the hands between the thighs (on the groin) facing upwards. –47.

नासाग्रे विन्यसेद्राजदन्तमूले तु जिह्वया ।

उत्तम्भ्य चिबुकं वक्षस्युत्थाप्य् पवनं शनैः ॥४८॥

nāsāgre vinyasedrājadantamūle tu jihvayā ।

uttambhya cibukaṃ vakṣasyutthāpya pavanaṃ śanaiḥ ॥48॥

Gaze at the tip of the nose, keeping the tongue pressed against the root of the upper teeth, press the chin against the chest and slowly raise the *prāṇa* upward. –48.

इदं पद्मासनं प्रोक्तं सर्वव्याधिविनाशनम् ।

दुर्लभं येन केनापि धीमता लभ्यते भुवि ॥४९॥

idāṃ padmāsanaṃ proktaṃ sarvavyādhivināśanam ।

durlabhaṃ yena kenāpi dhīmatā labhyate bhuvi ॥49॥

This is called *padmāsana*, the destroyer of all diseases. It cannot be gained by everyone; only some wise people achieve it on this earth. –49.

Padmāsana Awakens the Kuṇḍalinī Śakti

कृत्वा सम्पुटितौ करौ दृढतरं बद्ध्वा तु पद्ममासनं

गाढं वक्षसि सन्निधाय चिबुकं ध्यायंश्च तच्चेतसि ।

वारं वारमपानमूर्ध्वमनिलं प्रोत्सारयन्पूरितं

न्यञ्चन्प्राणमुपैति बोधमतुलं शक्तिप्रभावान्नरः ॥५०॥

kṛtvā sampuṭitau karau dṛḍhataraṃ baddhvā tu padmamāsanaṃ

gāḍhaṃ vakṣasi sannidhāya cibukaṃ dhyāyaṃśca taccetasi ।

vāraṃvāramapānamūrdhvamanilaṃ protsārayanpūritaṃ

nyañcanprāṇamupaiti bodhamatulaṃ śaktiprabhāvānnaraḥ ॥ *50* ॥

Steadfastly assuming the *padmāsana*, keeping one palm on the other and the chin fixed on the chest, concentrate the mind on *tat* (the Self). Repeatedly draw *apāna vāyu* (the vital air) upward and then push the inhaled *prāṇa* downward. Thus joining the *prāna* and *apāna* a man gets supreme knowledge and power by awakening the *Śakti* (*Kuṇḍalinī*). –50.

पद्मासने स्थितो योगी नाडीद्वारेण पूरितम् ।

मारुतं धारयेद्यस्तु स मुक्तो नात्र संशयः ॥५१॥

padmāsane sthito yogī nāḍīdvāreṇa pūritam ।

mārutaṃ dhārayedyastu sa mukto nātra saṃśayaḥ ॥*51* ॥

Being seated in *padmāsana*, the yogī who fills the *nāḍīs* (with the *prāṇa*) inhaling through their entrances (of the *nāḍīs* i.e. *idā* and *piṅgalā*), and restrains the *prāṇa* drawn in through the *nāḍīs*, achieves liberation. There is no doubt about it. –51.

Siṃhāsana (Lion's Pose)

अथ सिंहासनम् ।

गुल्फौ च वृषणस्याधः सीवन्त्याः पार्श्वयोः क्षिपेत् ।

दक्षिणे सव्यगुल्फं तु दक्षगुल्फं तु सव्यके ॥५२॥

atha siṃhāsanam ।

Now *simhāsana* is described.

gulphau ca vṛṣaṇasyādhaḥ sīvannyāḥ pārśvayoḥ kṣipet ।

dakṣiṇe savyagulphaṃ tu dakṣagulphaṃ tu savyake ॥*52* ॥

Place the ankles below the scrotum on the sides of the perineum, with the left ankle on the right side and right ankle on the left side (of the perineum). –52.

हस्तौ तु जान्वोः संस्थाप्य स्वाङ्गुलीः सम्प्रसार्य च ।

व्यात्तवक्तो निरीक्षेत नासाग्रं सुसमाहितः ॥५३॥

hastau tu jānvoḥ saṃsthāpya svāṅgulīḥ samprasārya ca ।

vyāttavaktro nirīkṣeta nāsāgraṃ susamāhitaḥ ॥53॥

Place the palms on the knees with the fingers extended apart and keep the mouth open. With a focused mind, gaze at the tip of the nose. –53.

सिंहासनं भवेदेतत्पूजितं योगिपुङ्गवैः ।

बन्धत्रितयसन्धानं कुरुते चासनोत्तमम् ॥५४॥

siṃhāsanaṃ bhavedetatpūjitaṃ yogipuṅgavaiḥ ।

bandhatritayasandhānaṃ kurute cāsanottamam ॥54॥

This is *siṃhāsana* highly appreciated by the greatest yogīs. This excellent *āsana* facilitates the concurrent practice of three *bandhas*. –54.

Bhadrāsana (Gracious Pose)

अथ भद्रासनम् ।

गुल्फौ च वृषणस्याधः सीवन्त्याः पार्श्वयोः क्षिपेत् ।

सव्यगुल्फं तथा सव्ये दक्षगुल्फं तु दक्षिणे ॥५५॥

atha bhadrāsanam ।

Now *bhadrāsana* is described.

gulphau ca vṛṣaṇasyādhaḥ sīvanyā pārśvayoḥ kṣipet ।

savyagulphaṃ tathā savye dakṣagulphaṃ tu dakṣiṇe ॥55॥

Place the ankles below the (area of) genitals on the sides of the perineum, the left ankle on the left side and the right ankle on the right side. –55.

पार्श्वपादौ च पाणिभ्यां दृढं बद्ध्वा सुनिश्चलम् ।

भद्रासनं भवेदेतत्सर्वव्याधिविनाशनम् ।

गोरक्षासनमित्याहुरिदं वै सिद्धयोगिनः ॥५६॥

pārśvapādau ca pāṇibhyāṃ dṛḍhaṃ baddhvā suniścalam ।

bhadrāsanaṃ bhavedetatsarvavyādhivināśanam ।

gorakṣāsanamityāhuridāṃ vai siddhayoginaḥ ॥56॥

Bind the feet firmly with the hands on each side and remain

quite motionless. This is *bhadrāsana* (the gentleman's pose), and it destroys all diseases. The perfected yogīs call it *gorakshāsana*. –56.

एवमासनबन्धेषु योगीन्द्रो विगतश्रमः ।

अभ्यसेन्नाडिकाशुद्धिं मुद्रादिपवनीक्रियाम् ॥५७॥

evamāsanabandheṣu yogīndro vigataśramaḥ ।

abhyasennāḍikāśuddhiṃ mudrādipavanakriyām ॥57॥

Thus the excellent yogīs, being free from tiredness during the practice of *āsanas* and *bandhas*, should practice purification of the *nāḍīs* as well as *mudrās* and techniques of *prāṇāyāma*. –57.

Sequence of Practice in Haṭha Yoga

आसनं कुम्भकं चित्रं मुद्राख्यं करणं तथा ।

अथ नादानुसन्धानमभ्यासानुक्रमो हठे ॥५८॥

āsanaṃ kumbhakaṃ citraṃ mudrākhyaṃ karaṇaṃ tathā ।

atha nādānusandhānamabhyāsānākramo haṭhe ॥58॥

Āsanas, the various *kumbhakas*, the means of practices called *mudrās* and *nādānusandhāna* (exploration of the inner mystical sound) form the order of practice in *Haṭha Yoga*. –58.

ब्रह्मचारी मिताहारी त्यागी योगपरायणः ।

अब्दादूर्ध्वं भवेद्सिद्धो नात्र कार्या विचारणा ॥५९॥

brahmacārī mitāhārī tyāgī yogaparāyaṇaḥ ।

abdādūrdhvaṃ bhavetsiddho nātra kāryā vicāraṇā ॥59॥

One who leads a celibate life, takes a moderate diet, renounces attachment to sensual pleasures, and is fully devoted to yoga, attains perfection over a year's practice. There is no doubt about it. –59.

About Mitāhāra – Moderate Diet

सुस्निग्धमधुराहारश्चतुर्थांशविवर्जितः ।

भुज्यते शिवसम्प्रीत्यै मिताहारः स उच्यते ॥६०॥

susnigdhamadhurāhāraścaturthāṃśavivarjitaḥ ।

bhujyate śivasamprītyai mitāhāraḥ sa ucyate ॥60॥

Definition of a moderate diet is: taking sweet and pleasant food (that is wholesome and natural), leaving one-quarter of the stomach empty and eating the food as an offering to please *Śiva*. –60.

कट्वाम्लतीक्ष्णलवणोष्णहरीतशाक-

सौवीरतैलतिलसर्षपमद्यमत्स्यान् ।

आजादिमांसदधितक्रकुलत्थकोल

पिण्याकहिङ्गुलशुनाद्यमपथ्यमाहुः ॥६१॥

kaṭvāmlatīkṣṇalavaṇoṣṇaharītaśāka-

sauvīratailatilasarṣapamadyamatsyān ।

ājādimāṃsadadhitakrakulatthakola

piṇyākahiṅgulaśunādyamapathyamāhuḥ ॥61॥

The following foods are considered to be unwholesome for the yogīs: those which are bitter, sour, pungent, salty, hot, green vegetables (other than those permitted ones), sour wheat or barley-gruel, oil, sesame and mustard, alcohol, fish, flesh of animals such as goats, etc., curd, buttermilk, horse gram, fruit of the jujube, oil cakes, asafoetidā and garlic. –61.

भोजनमहितं विद्यात्पुनरस्योष्णीकृतं रूक्षम् ।

अतिलवणमम्लयुक्तं कदशनशाकोत्कं वर्ज्यम् ॥६२॥

bhojanamahitaṃ vidyātpunarasyoṣṇīkṛtaṃ rūkṣam ।

atilavaṇamamlayuktaṃ kadaśanaśākotkataṃ varjyam ॥62॥

The following diet should be known as unhealthy, and be avoided: food that is once cooked and heated again, food that is dry, too salty or acidic, stale or has too many vegetables. –62.

वह्निस्त्रीपथिसेवानामादौ वर्जनमाचरेत् ।

तथा हि गोरक्षवचनम् ।

वर्जयेद्दुर्जनप्रान्तं वह्निस्त्रीपथिसेवनम् ।

प्रातःस्नानोपवासादि कायक्लेशविधिं तथा ॥६३॥

vahnistrīpathisevānāmādau varjanamācaret ।

tathā hi gorakṣavacanam ।

"varjayeddurjanaprāntaṃ vahni strīpathisevanam ।

prātaḥsnānopavāsādikāyakleśavidhiṃ tathā" ॥63॥

Sitting near a fire, having sexual relations with women and traveling (long distances) should be avoided in the beginning. Therefore, *Gorakṣanātha* said these words: the company of evil people, sexual relations, bathing early in the morning, fasting, and hard physical work should be avoided. –63.

गोधूमशालियवषाष्टिकशोभनान्नं

क्षीराज्यखण्डनवनीतसिद्धामधूनि ।

शुण्ठीपटोलकफलादिकपञ्चशाकं

मुद्गादिदिव्यमुदकं च यमीन्द्रपथ्यम् ॥६४॥

godhūmaśāliyavaṣāṣṭikaśobhanānnaṃ-

kṣīrājyakhaṇḍanavanītasitāmadhūni ।

śuṇṭhīpaṭolakaphalādikapañcaśākaṃ

mudgādidivyamudakaṃ ca yamīndrapathyam ॥64॥

The wholesome foods for the yogī are: wheat, rice, good grains, milk, ghee, brown sugar, (sugar candy), butter, honey, dry ginger, cucumber, five vegetables, *muṅa* (green gram – phaseolus radiatus) and similar pulses, and pure water. –64.

पुष्टं सुमधुरं स्निग्धं गव्यं धातुप्रपोषणम् ।

मनोभिलषितं योग्यं योगी भोजनमाचरेत् ॥६५॥

puṣṭaṃ sumadhuraṃ snigdhaṃ gavyaṃ dhātupraposaṇam ।

mano'bhilaṣitaṃ yogyaṃ yogī bhojanamācaret ॥65॥

The yogī should take nourishing and sweet food mixed with ghee and milk; it should be appealing to his mind and nourish the *dhātus* (essential constituents or ingredients of the body). –65.

Perfection Through Practice Alone

युवो वृद्धोऽतिवृद्धो वा व्याधितो दुर्बलोऽपि वा ।

अभ्यासात्सिद्धिमाप्नोति सर्वयोगेष्वतन्द्रितः ॥६६॥

yuvā vṛddho'tivṛddho vā vyādhito durbalo'pi vā ।

abhyāsātsiddhimāpnoti sarvayogeṣvatandritaḥ ॥66॥

Whether young or old, even very old, sick or weak, one can attain perfection in all the yogas through active practice. –66.

क्रियायुक्तस्य सिद्धिः स्यादक्रियस्य कथं भवेत् ।

न शास्त्रपाठमात्रेण योगसिद्धिः प्रजायते ॥६७॥

kriyāyuktasya siddhiḥ syādakriyasya kathaṃ bhavet ।

na śāstrapāṭhamātreṇa yogasiddhiḥ prajāyate ॥67॥

One attains perfection by uniting oneself with *kriyā* (i.e. through right practice). How can it be gained by someone who does not practice? Perfection in yoga can never be attained by merely reading the *śāstras* (religious texts or scriptures). –67.

न वेषधारणं सिद्धेः कारणं न च तत्कथा ।

क्रियैव कारणं सिद्धेः सत्यमेतन्न संशयः ॥६८॥

na veṣadhāraṇaṃ siddheḥ kāraṇaṃ na ca tatkathā ।

kriyaiva kāraṇaṃ siddheḥ satyametanna saṃśayaḥ ॥68॥

Perfection cannot be attained by wearing a dress of a yogī or by talking about (the various means of) yoga. Practice alone is the means of perfection. This is the truth and there is no doubt about it. –68.

पीठानि कुम्भकाश्चित्रा दिव्यानि करणानि च ।

सर्वाण्यपि हठाभ्यासे राजयोगफलावधि ॥६९॥

pīṭhāni kumbhakāścitrā divyāni karaṇāni ca ।

sarvāṇyapi haṭhābhyāse rājayogaphalāvadhi ॥69॥

Āsanas, various types of *kumbhakas* as well as various others divine means should also be practiced in *Haṭha Yoga* until the fruit of *Rāja* Yoga is attained. –69.

इति हठयोगप्रदीपिकायां प्रथमोपदेशः ॥

iti haṭhayogapradīpikāyāṃ prathamopadeśaḥ ||

Thus ends the Chapter One of *Haṭha Yoga Pradīpikā.*

CHAPTER TWO

द्वितीयोपदेशः

Discourse on Prāṇāyāma

Description of Prāṇāyāma

अथासने दृढे योगी वशी हितमिताशनः ।

गुरूपदिष्टमार्गेण प्राणायामान्समभ्यसेत् ॥१॥

athāsane dṛdhe yogī vaśī hitamitāśanaḥ ।

gurūpadiṣṭamārgeṇa prāṇāyāmān samabhyaset ॥1॥

After having mastered the *āsanas*, the yogī, having his senses and body under control, taking a wholesome and moderate diet, should practice *prāṇāyāma* according to the instructions of his guru. –1.

चले वाते चलं चित्तं निश्चले निश्चलं भवेत् ॥

योगी स्थाणुत्वमाप्नोति ततो वायुं निरोधयेत् ॥२॥

cale vāte calaṃ cittaṃ niścale niścalaṃ bhavet ।

yogī sthāṇutvamāpnoti tato vāyuṃ nirodhayet ॥2॥

When the breath (*prāṇa*) wanders or becomes irregular, the mind also moves or becomes unstable. When the breath is still, the mind is also steady. Through the stillness of breath, the yogī attains steadiness of the mind. Therefore, the yogī should restrain the *vāyu* (vital air). –2.

यावद्वायुः स्थितो देहे तावज्जीवनमुच्यते ।

मरणं तस्य निष्क्रान्तिस्ततो वायुं निरोधयेत् ॥३॥

yāvadvāyuḥ sthito dehe tāvajjīvanamucyate ।

maraṇaṃ tasya niṣkrāntistato vāyuṃ nirodhayet ॥3॥

So long as the *vāyu* (*prāṇa*) remains in the body, it is called life. When the *prāṇa* leaves the body, this is death. Therefore, one should restrain the *vāyu*. –3.

मलाकलासु नाडीषु मारुतो नैव मध्यगः ।

कथं स्यादुन्मनीभावः कार्यसिद्धिः कथं भवेत् ॥४॥

malākulāsu nāḍīṣu māruto naiva madhyagaḥ ।

kathaṃ syādunmanībhāvaḥ kāryasiddhiḥ kathaṃ bhavet ॥4॥

The *maruta* (vital air) does not pass through the middle channel (*suṣumṇā*) due to the numerous impurities in the *nāḍīs* (psychic pathways). Therefore, how can there be the state of *unmanī* (the state beyond the mind) and how can perfection be attained? –4.

Purification of Nāḍīs

शुद्धमेति यदा सर्वं नाडी-चक्रं मलाकुलम् ।

तदैव जायते योगी प्राणसंग्रहणे क्षमः ॥५॥

śuddhimeti yadā sarvaṃ nāḍīcakraṃ malākulam ।

tadaiva jāyate yogī prāṇasanggrahaṇe kṣamaḥ ॥5॥

Only when all the *nāḍīs* and *cakras* (psychic energy centers) that are full of impurities are purified, would the yogī be able to restrain the *prāṇa*. –5.

प्राणायामं ततः कुर्यान्नित्यं सात्त्विकया धिया ।

यथा सुषुम्णानाडीस्था मलाः शुद्धिं प्रयान्ति च ॥६॥

prāṇāyāmaṃ tataḥ kuryānnityaṃ sāttvikayā dhiyā ।

yathā suṣumṇānāḍīsthā malāḥ śuddhiṃ prayānti ca ॥6॥

Therefore, *prāṇāyāma* should be performed daily with a *sattvic* (pure) state of mind until the impurities of the *suṣumṇā nāḍī* are eliminated. –6.

Alternate Nostril Breathing

बद्धपद्मासनो योगी प्राणं चन्द्रेण पूरयेत् ।

धारयित्वा यथाशक्ति भूयः सूर्येण रेचयेत् ॥७॥

baddhapadmāsano yogī prāṇaṃ candreṇa pūrayet ।

dhārayitvā yathāśakti bhūyaḥ sūryeṇa recayet ॥7॥

Sitting firmly in the *padmāsana* posture, the yogī should inhale through the *candra* (left nostril) and retain the breath inside as long as possible. Then exhale it through the *sūrya* (right nostril). –7.

प्राणं सूर्येण चाकृष्य पूरयेदुदरं शनैः ।

विधिवत्कुम्भकं कृत्वा पुनश्चन्द्रेण रेचयेत् ॥८॥

prāṇaṃ sūryeṇa cākṛṣya pūrayedudaraṃ śanaiḥ ।

vidhivatkumbhakaṃ kṛtvā punaścandreṇa recayet ॥8॥

Then, inhaling through the *sūrya* (right nostril), slowly fill the belly, and after properly performing the *kumbhaka* (retention), exhale through the *candra* (left nostril). –8.

येन त्यजेत्तेन पीत्वा धारयेदतिरोधतः ।

रेचयेच्च ततोऽन्येन शनैरेव न वेगतः ॥९॥

yena tyajettena pītvā dhārayedatirodhataḥ ।

recayecca tato'nyena śanaireva na vegataḥ ॥9॥

Then inhale through the same nostril through which exhalation was just performed, hold the breath as long as possible, and exhale it slowly, not forcibly through the other nostril. –9.

प्राणं चेदिडया पिबेन्नियमितं भूयोऽन्यथा रेचयेत्

पीत्वा पिङ्गलया समीरणमथो बद्ध्वा त्यजेद्वामया ।

सूर्यचन्द्रमसोरनेन विधिनाभ्यासं सदा तन्वतां

शुद्धा नाडिगणा भवन्ति यमिनां मासत्रयादूर्ध्वतः ॥१०॥

prāṇaṃ cediḍayā pibenniyamitaṃ bhūyo'nyayā recayet

pītvā piṅgalayā samīraṇamatho baddhvā tyajedvāmayā ।

sūryacandramasoranena vidhinā'bhyāsaṃ sadā tanvatāṃ

śuddhā nāḍigaṇā bhavanti yamināṃ māsatrayādūrdhvataḥ ॥10॥

If the *prāṇa* is inhaled through the left nostril, then it should be regulated by exhaling through the opposite nostril. After inhaling through the right, hold it inside and exhale it through the left. By practicing constantly in this way through the right and left nostrils alternatively, all the *nāḍīs* of the *yami* are purified over a period of three months. –10.

Time of Practice

प्रातर्मध्यन्दिने सायमर्धरात्रे च कुम्भकान् ।

शनैरशीतिपर्यन्तं चतुर्वारं समभ्यसेत् ॥११॥

prātarmadhyadine sāyamardharātre ca kumbhakān ।

śanairaśītiparyantaṃ caturvāraṃ samabhyaset ॥11॥

Kumbhaka (retention of breath) should be performed four times a day: morning, midday, evening and midnight. The number of *kumbhakas* should gradually increase up to eighty counts (in one sitting). –11.

कनीयसि भवेद्स्वेद कम्पो भवति मध्यमे ।

उत्तमे स्थानमाप्नोति ततो वायुं निबन्धयेत् ॥१२॥

kanīyasi bhavedsvedah kampo bhavati madhyame ।

uttame sthānamāpnoti tato vāyuṃ nibandhayet ॥12॥

In the first stage, the body (of the yogī) perspires. In the second stage, his body trembles. In the highest stage, the yogī gains steadiness. Therefore, the *vāyu (prāṇa)* should be withheld. –12.

जलेन श्रमजातेन गात्रमर्दनमाचरेत् ।

दृढता लघुता चैव तेन गात्रस्य जायते ॥१३॥

jalena śramajātena gātramardanamācaret ।

dṛḍhatā laghutā caiva tena gātrasya jāyate ॥13॥

The perspiration coming from the exertion of *prāṇāyāma* practice should be rubbed on the body. This gives firmness and lightness to the physical constitution. –13

Practice of Prāṇāyāma and Diet

अभ्यासकाले प्रथमे शस्तं क्षीराज्यभोजनम् ।
ततोऽभ्यासे दृढीभूते न तादृङ्नियमग्रहः ॥१४॥

abhyāsakāle prathame śastaṃ kṣīrājyabhojanam ।
tato'bhyāse dṛḍhībhūte na tādṛṅniyamagrahaḥ ॥14॥

In the early stages of practice, food containing milk and ghee is best. When one is well established in his practice, then he needs not observe these restrictions. –14.

यथा सिंहो गजो व्याघ्रो भवेद्वश्यः शनैः शनैः ।
तथैव सेवितो वायुरन्यथा हन्ति साधकम् ॥१५॥

yathā siṃho gajo vyāghro bhavedvaśyaḥ śanaiḥ śanaiḥ ।
tathaiva sevito vāyuranyathā hanti sādhakam ॥15॥

Just as lions, elephants and tigers are gradually brought under control, so should be done with the *prāṇa*. Otherwise, it can kill the practitioner. –15.

Destruction of Diseases

प्राणायामेन युक्तेन सर्वरोगक्षयो भवेत् ।
अयुक्ताभ्यासयोगेन सर्वरोगसमुद्गमः ॥१६॥

prāṇāyāmādiyuktena sarvarogakṣayo bhavet ।
ayuktābhyāsayogena sarvarogasamudbhavaḥ ॥16॥

Through proper practice of *prāṇāyāma* (along with other practices like moderate diet etc.) all diseases are destroyed. Through improper practice of yoga, however, all types of diseases are generated. –16.

हिक्का श्वासश्च कासश्च शिरःकर्णाक्षिवेदनाः ।
भवन्ति विविधाः रोगाः पवनस्य प्रकोपतः ॥१७॥

hikkā śvāsaśca kāsaśca śiraḥkarṇākṣivedanāḥ ।
bhavanti vividhā rogāḥ pavanasya prakopataḥ ॥17॥

Hiccups, asthma, coughs, headaches, ear and eye pain, and various other diseases are generated due to disturbances of the vital air. –17.

Proper Practice Needed for Perfection

युक्तं युक्तं त्यजेद्वायुं युक्तं युक्तं च पूरयेत् ।

युक्तं युक्तं च बध्नीयादेवं सिद्धिमवाप्नुयात् ॥१८॥

yuktaṃ yuktaṃ tyajedvāyuṃ yuktaṃ yuktaṃ ca pūrayet ।

yuktaṃ yuktaṃ ca badhnīyādevaṃ siddhimavāpnuyāt ॥18॥

The *vāyu* should be skillfully inhaled, skillfully exhaled and skillfully retained in order to attain perfection. –18.

यदा तु नाडीशुद्धिः स्यात्तथा चिह्नानि बाह्यतः ।

कायस्य कृशता कान्तिस्तदा जायते निश्चितम् ॥१९॥

yadā tu nāḍīśuddhiḥ syāttathācinhāni bāhyataḥ ।

kāyasya kṛśatā kāntistadā jāyeta niścitam ॥19॥

When the *nāḍīs* are purified, there appear some external signs (of success). One certain result is that the body becomes slender and bright. –19.

यथेष्टं धारणं वायोरनलस्य प्रदीपनम् ।

नादाभिव्यक्तिरारोग्यं जायते नाडिशोधनात् ॥२०॥

yatheṣṭadhāraṇaṃ vāyoranalasya pradīpanam ।

nādābhivyaktirārogyaṃ jāyate nāḍiśodhanāt ॥20॥

When the yoga practitioner is able to hold the *vāyu* as desired, the digestive fire is stimulated. Through the purification of the *nāḍīs*, the *nāda* (inner sound) is heard and good heath is attained. –20.

Description of Ṣaṭkarma – Six Cleansing Practices

मेदश्लेष्माधिकः पूर्वं षट्कर्माणि समाचरेत् ।

अन्यस्तु नाचरेत्तानि दोषाणां समभावतः ॥२१॥

medaśleṣmādhikaḥ pūrvaṃ ṣaṭkarmāṇi samācaret ।

anyastu nācarettāni doṣāṇāṃ samabhāvataḥ ॥21॥

When there is an excess of fat or mucus (in the body),

the *ṣaṭkarma* (six cleansing acts) should be performed first. Others should not go through these acts (of cleansing) if the three humors *vāta*, *pitta* and *kapha* (the wind, bile and mucus) are balanced in the body. –21.

धौतिर्बस्तिस्तथा नेतिस्त्राटकं नौलिकं तथा ।

कपालभातिश्चैतानि षट्कर्माणि प्रचक्षते ॥२२॥

dhautirbastistathā netistrāṭakaṃ naulikaṃ tathā ।

kapālabhātiścaitāni ṣaṭkarmāṇi pracakṣate ॥22॥

Dhauti, basti, neti, trāṭaka, nauli and *kapālabhāti* are known *ṣaṭkarma* (six yogic cleansing acts). –22.

कर्म षट्कमिदं गोप्यं घटशोधनकारकम् ।

विचित्रगुणसन्धाय पूज्यते योगिपुङ्गवैः ॥२३॥

karma ṣaṭkamidāṃ gopyaṃ ghaṭaśodhanakārakam ।

vicitraguṇasandhāyi pūjyate yogipuṅgavaiḥ ॥23॥

These *ṣaṭkarma* which act for the purification of the body are secret. They give various wonderful results and are highly cherished by the great yogīs. –23.

Practice of Dhauti – Internal Cleansing

अथ धौतिः ।

चतुर्अङ्गुलविस्तारं हस्तपञ्चदशायतम् ।

गुरूपदिष्टमार्गेण सिक्तं वस्त्रं शनैर्ग्रसेत् ।

पुनः प्रत्याहरेच्चैतदुदितं धौतिकर्म तत् ॥२४॥

atha dhautiḥ ।

Now *dhauti* is described.

caturaṅgulavistāraṃ hastapañcadaśāyatam ।

gurūpadiṣṭamārgeṇa siktaṃ vastraṃ śanairgraset ।

punaḥ pratyāhareccaitaduditaṃ dhautikarma tat ॥24॥

A strip of wet cloth, with four fingers wide and fifteen-hand spans long, is gradually swallowed down and slowly removed, according to the instructions of the guru. This is called *dhauti karma*. –24.

कासश्वासप्लीहकुष्ठं कफरोगाश्च विंशतिः ।

धौतिकर्मप्रभावेण प्रयान्त्येव न संशयः ॥२५॥

kāsaśvāsaplīhakuṣṭhaṃ kapharogāśca viṃśatiḥ ।

dhautikarmaprabhāveṇa prayāntyeva na saṃśayaḥ ॥25॥

Coughs, asthma, diseases of the spleen, leprosy and twenty other mucus related diseases are removed by the practice of *dhauti karma*. –25.

Practice of Basti – Yogic Enema

अथ बस्तिः ।

नाभिदघ्नजले पायौ न्यस्तनालोत्कटासनः ।

आधाराकुञ्चनं कुर्यात्क्षालनं बस्तिकर्म तत् ॥२६॥

atha bastiḥ ।

Now *basti* is described.

nābhidāghrājale pāyau nyastanālotkaṭāsanaḥ ।

ādhārākuñcanaṃ kuryātkṣālanaṃ bastikarma tat ॥26॥

Sit in *utkatāsana* in navel deep water, insert a (fine soft) tube into the anus, contract it (to draw water in), and wash (thoroughly) inside (the colon). This is called *basti karma*. –26.

गुल्मप्लीहोदरं चापि वातपित्तकफोद्भवाः ।

बस्तिकर्मप्रभावेण क्षीयन्ते सकलामयाः ॥२७॥

gulmaplīhodaraṃ cāpi vātapittakaphodbhavāḥ ।

bastikarmaprabhāveṇa kṣīyante sakalāmayāḥ ॥27॥

The power of the *basti karma* can cure enlarged glands and spleen and will destroy all diseases arising from (imbalances of) the wind, bile and mucus. –27.

धान्त्वद्रियान्तःकरणप्रसादं दधाच्च कान्तिं दहनप्रदीप्तम् ।

अशेषदोषोपचयं निहन्याद् अभ्यस्यमानं जलबस्तिकर्म ॥२८॥

dhātvindriyāntaḥkaraṇaprasādaṃ

dadhācca kāntiṃ dahanapradīptam ।

aśeṣadoṣopacayaṃ nihanyād

abhyasyamānaṃ jalabastikarma ॥28॥

By the practice of *basti* the digestive fire increases, the body glows, the entire excess of humors accumulated in the bodily constitution are destroyed and the *dhātu* (physical constituents), senses and mind (of the practitioner) are purified. –28.

Practice of Neti – Nasal Cleansing

अथ नेतिः ।

सूत्रं वितस्तिसुस्निग्धं नासानाले प्रवेशयेत् ।

मुखान्निर्गमयेच्चैषा नेतिः सिद्धैर्निगद्यते ॥२९॥

atha netiḥ ।

Now *neti* is described.

sūtraṃ vitasti susnigdhaṃ nāsānāle praveśayet ।

mukhānnirgamayeccaiṣā netiḥ siddhairnigadyate ॥29॥

Insert a fairly soft thread, twelve fingers long, through the nose and take it out through the mouth. This is called *neti* by the *siddhas*. –29.

कपालशोधिनी चैव दिव्यदृष्टिप्रदायिनी ।

जत्रूर्ध्वजातरोगौघं नेतिराशु निहन्ति च ॥३०॥

kapālaśodhinī caiva divyadṛṣṭipradāyinī ।

jatrūrdhvajātarogaughaṃ netirāśu nihanti ca ॥30॥

Neti cleanses the skull (cranium) and gives divine vision. All diseases that arise above the clavicle are also quickly destroyed by the practice of *neti*. –30.

Practice of Trāṭaka – Concentrated Gazing

अथ त्राटकम् ।

निरीक्षेन्निश्चलदृशा सूक्ष्मलक्ष्यं समाहितः ।

अश्रुसम्पातपर्यन्तमाचार्यैस्त्राटकं स्मृतम् ॥३१॥

atha trāṭakam ।

Now *trāṭaka* is described.

nirīkṣenniścaladṛśā sūkṣmalakṣyaṃ samāhitaḥ ।

aśrusampātaparyantamācāryaistrāṭakaṃ smṛtam ॥31॥

Gaze steadily at a small object with a concentrated mind until tears start shedding (out of the eyes). This is known as *trāṭaka* by the masters of yoga. –31.

मोचनं नेत्ररोगाणां तन्द्रादीणां कपाटकम् ।

यत्नतस्त्राटकं गोप्यं यथा हाटकपेटकम् ॥३२॥

mocanaṃ netrarogāṇāṃ tandrādīṇāṃ kapāṭakam ।

yatnatastrāṭakaṃ gopyaṃ yathā hāṭakapeṭakam ॥32॥

Trāṭaka frees one from all diseases of the eye, removes fatigue and drowsiness, and blocks the doorway to these problems. So, it should be carefully kept secret like a golden box. –32.

Practice of Nauli – Abdominal Rotation

अथ नौलिः ।

अमन्दावर्तवेगेन तुन्दं सव्यापसव्यतः ।

नतांसो भ्रामयेदेषा नौलिः सिद्धैः प्रशस्यते ॥३३॥

atha nauliḥ ।

Now *nauli* is described.

amandāvartavegena tundaṃ savyāpasavyataḥ ।

natāṃso bhrāmayedeṣā nauliḥ siddhaiḥ praśasyate ॥33॥

Bending the body forward, bulge out the belly and rotate it from right to left and vice versa. This is *nauli*, praised by the *siddhas*. –33.

मन्दाग्निसन्दीपनपाचनादिसन्धापिकानन्दकरी सदैव ।

अशेषदोषमयशोषणी च हठक्रिया मौलिरियं च नौलिः॥३४॥

mandāgnisandīpanapācanādi-

sandhāpikānandakarī sadaiva ।

aśeṣa doṣamayaśoṣaṇī ca

haṭhakriyāmauliriyaṃ ca nauliḥ ॥34॥

Nauli is the crown of *Haṭha Yoga* practice. It stimulates sluggish digestive fire and removes indigestion. It destroys all diseases, and disorders of the *doṣas* (imbalances of the three humors – bile, wind and mucus) and always brings about happiness. –34.

Kapālabhāti - Frontal Brain Cleansing

अथ कपालभातिः ।

भस्त्रावल्लोहकारस्य रेचपूरौ ससम्भ्रमौ ।

कपालभातिर्विख्याता कफदोषविशोषणी ॥३५॥

atha kapālabhātiḥ ।

Now *kapālabhāti* is described.

bhastrāvallohakārasya recapūrau sasambhramau ।

kapālabhātirvikhyātā kaphadoṣaviśoṣaṇī ॥35॥

Perform *recaka* (exhalation) and *pūraka* (inhalation) rapidly like the bellows of a blacksmith. This is called *kapālabhāti*, and it destroys all the diseases (resulting from the imbalances) of the *kapha* (phlegm). –35.

Ṣaṭkarma Removes Impurities

षट्कर्मनिर्गतस्थौल्यकफदोषमलादिकः ।

प्राणायामं ततः कुर्यादनायासेन सिद्ध्यति ॥३६॥

ṣaṭkarmanirgatasthaulyakaphadoṣamalādikaḥ ।

prāṇāyāmaṃ tataḥ kuryādanāyāsena siddhyati ॥36॥

Through the practice of the *ṣaṭkarmas*, one is freed from excesses of fat, mucus and other impurities. Then *prāṇāyāma* should be practiced and perfection will be attained without difficulty. –36.

प्राणायामैरेव सर्वे प्रशुष्यन्ति मला इति ।

आचार्याणां तु केषांचिदन्यत्कर्म न संमतम् ॥३७॥

prāṇāyāmaireva sarve praśuṣyanti malā iti ।

ācāryāṇāṃ tu keṣāñcidānyatkarma na saṃmatam ॥37॥

According to (the opinion of) some *Haṭha Yoga* masters, *prāṇāyāma* by itself will remove all the impurities (of the body). So, they do not hold the other karmas (yogic cleansing acts) in high esteem. –37.

Gaja Karaṇī – Stomatch Cleansing

अथ गजकरणी ।

उदरगतपदार्थमुद्वमन्ति पवनमपानमुदीर्य कण्ठनाले ।

क्रमपरिचयवश्यनाडिचक्रा गजकरणीति निगद्यते हठज्ञैः ॥ ३८॥

atha gajakaraṇī ।

Now *gaja karaṇī* is described.

udaragatapadārthamudvamanti

pavanamapānamudīrya kaṇṭhanāle ।

kramaparicayavaśyanāḍicakrā

gajakaraṇīti nigadyate haṭhajñaiḥ ॥38॥

Vomit the contents of the stomach by drawing the *apāna* vāyu up to the throat. This practice gradually brings the *nāḍīs* and *cakras* under control. Thus, it is called *gaja karaṇī* by the wise and learned men of *Haṭha Yoga*. –38.

Prāṇāyāma Removes Fear of Death

ब्रह्मादयोऽपि त्रिदशाः पवनाभ्यासतत्पराः ।

अभूवन्नन्तकभ्यात्तस्मात्पवनमभ्यसेत् ॥ ३९॥

brahmādayo'pi tridāśāḥ pavanābhyāsatatparāḥ ।

abhūvannantakabhayāttasmātpavanamabhyaset ॥39॥

Even *Brahmā* (the Creator) and thirty-three other gods eagerly devoted themselves to the practice of *prāṇāyāma*, and were freed from the fear of death. Therefore, one should practice *prāṇāyāma*. –39.

Practice of Kumbhaka with

Śāmbhavī Mudrā

यावद्बद्धो मरुद्देशे यावच्चित्तं निराकुलम् ।

यावद्दृष्टिर्भ्रुवोर्मध्ये तावत्कालभयं कुतः ॥४०॥

yāvadbaddho maruddehe yāvaccittaṃ nirākulam ।

yāvaddṛṣṭirbhruvormadhye tāvatkālabhayaṃ kutaḥ ॥40॥

So long as the *prāṇa* is restrained in the body, the mind is steady and the gaze is focused between the two eyebrows, why should there be fear of death? –40.

विधिवत्प्राणसंयामैर्नाडीचक्रे विशोधिते ।

सुषुम्णावदनं भित्त्वा सुखाद्विशति मारुतः ॥४१॥

vidhivatprāṇasaṃyāmairnāḍīcakre viśodhite ।

suṣumṇāvadanaṃ bhittvā sukhādviśati mārutaḥ ॥41॥

With a systematic control of *prāṇa* when the *nāḍīs* and *cakras* are purified, the *muruta* (*prāṇa*) piercing the mouth of *suṣumṇā* may easily enter it. –41.

Manonmanī – Thoughtless State of Mind

अथ मनोन्मनी ।

मारुते मध्यसंचारे मनःस्थैर्यं प्रजायते ।

यो मनःसुस्थिरीभावः सैवावस्था मनोन्मनी ॥४२॥

atha manonmanī ।

Now *manonmanī* is described.

mārute madhyasañcāre manaḥsthairyaṃ prajāyate ।

yo manaḥ susthirībhāvaḥ saivāvasthā manonmanī ॥42॥

When the breath (*prāṇa*) moves through the middle passage, it makes the mind steady. This steadiness of the mind brings forth the state of *manonmanī* (state of *samādhi*). –42.

तत्सिद्धये विधानज्ञाश्चित्रान्कुर्वन्ति कुम्भकान् ।

विचित्र कुम्भकाभ्यासाद्विचित्रां सिद्धिमाप्नुयात् ॥४३॥

tatsiddhaye vidhānajñāścitrānkurvanti kumbhakān ।

vicitrakumbhakābhyāsādvicitrāṃ siddhimāpnuyāt ||43||

In order to attain (the previously described) *siddhi* (perfection), the wise ones perform various types of *kumbhakas*. They attain amazing *siddhis* through the practice of various *kumbhakas*. –43.

The Eight Kumbhaka Practices

अथ कुम्भकभेदाः ।

सूर्यभेदनमुज्जायी सीत्कारी शीतली तथा ।

भस्त्रिका भ्रामरी मूर्च्छा प्लाविनीत्यष्टकुम्भकाः ॥४४॥

atha kumbhakabhedāḥ ।

Now the types of *kumbhakas* are described.

sūryabhedanamujjāyī sītkārī śītalī tathā ।

bhastrikā bhrāmarī mūrcchā plāvinītyaṣṭakumbhakāḥ ||44||

The eight *kumbhakas* are *sūryaveda*, *ujjāyī*, *sītkārī*, *śītalī*, *bhastrikā*, *bhrāmarī*, *mūrcchā* and *plāvinī*. – 44.

Practice of Prāṇāyāma with Bandhas

पूरकान्ते तु कर्तव्यो बन्धो जालन्धराभिधः ।

कुम्भकान्ते रेचकादौ कर्तव्यस्तूड्डियानकः ॥४५॥

pūrakānte tu kartavyo bandho jālandharābhidhaḥ ।

kumbhakānte recakādau kartavyastūḍḍiyānakaḥ ||45||

At the end of inhalation, *jālandhara bandha* should be performed. At the end of retention (*kumbhaka*) and in the beginning of exhalation, *uḍḍiyāna bandha* should be practiced. –45.

अधस्तात्कुञ्चनेनाशु कण्ठसङ्कोचने कृते ।

मध्ये पश्चिमतानेन स्यात्प्राणो ब्रह्मनाडिगः ॥४६॥

adhastātkuñcanenāśu kaṇṭhasaṅkocane kṛte ।

madhye paścimatānena syātprāṇo brahmanāḍigaḥ ||67||

Contract the perineum (*mūla bandha*) quickly and the throat (*jālandhara bandha*) simultaneously, and draw back the center of abdomen (navel area). It causes the *prāṇa* to flow into the *brah-*

ma nāḍī (literally, psychic pathway that leads to *Brahma*). –46.

आपानमूर्ध्वमुत्थाप्य प्राणं कण्ठादधो नयेत् ।

योगी जराविमुक्तः सन्षोडशाब्दवया भवेत् ॥४७॥

āpānamūrdhvamutthāpya prāṇaṃ kaṇṭhādadho nayet ।

yogī jarāvimuktaḥ sanṣoḍaśābdavayo bhavet ॥47॥

By raising the *apāna vāyu* upwards (by contracting the perineum) and forcing the *prāṇa* downwards from the throat, the yogī is free from old age and becomes like a youth of sixteen. –47.

Practice of Sūryabheda Prāṇāyāma

अथ सूर्यभेदनम् ।

आसने सुखदे योगी बद्ध्वा चैवासनं ततः ।

दक्षनाड्या समाकृष्य बहिःस्थं पवनं शनैः ॥४८॥

atha sūryabhedanam ।

Now *sūryabhedana* is described.

āsane sukhade yogī baddhvā caivāsanaṃ tataḥ ।

dakṣanāḍyā samākṛṣya bahiḥsthaṃ pavanaṃ śanaiḥ ॥48॥

Sitting in a comfortable pose, the yogī should stabilize himself in the posture and then slowly draw the breath in through the right nostril. –48.

आकेशादानखाग्राच्च निरोधावधि कुम्भयेत् ।

ततः शनैः सव्यनाड्या रेचयेत्पवनं शनैः ॥४९॥

ākeśādānakhāgrācca nirodhāvadhi kumbhayet ।

tataḥ śanaiḥ savyanāḍyā recayetpavanaṃ śanaiḥ ॥49॥

Kumbhaka should be performed until the *prāṇa* pervades the whole body from the top of the head to the tips of the toes. Then it should slowly be exhaled through the right nostril. –49.

कपालशोधनं वातदोषघ्नं कृमिदोषहृत् ।

पुनः पुनरिदं कार्यं सूर्यभेदनमुत्तमम् ॥५०॥

kapālaśodhanaṃ vātadoṣaghnaṃ kṛmidoṣahṛt ।

punaḥ punaridāṃ kāryaṃ sūryabhedanamuttamam ॥50॥

This *prāṇāyāma* purifies the cranium and destroys diseases arising from the imbalances of the *vāta* (wind). It also eliminates infestation by parasites (worms etc.). This excellent *sūrya bheda prāṇāyāma* should be performed repeatedly. –50.

Practice of Ujjāyī – Psychic Breathing

अथ उज्जायी ।

मुखं संयम्य नाडीभ्यामाकृष्य पवनं शनैः ।

यथा लगति कण्ठात्तु हृदयावधि सस्वनम् ॥५१॥

athojjāyī ।

Now *ujjāyī* is described.

mukhaṃ saṃyamya nāḍībhyāmākṛṣya pavanaṃ śanaiḥ ।

yathā lagati kaṇṭhāttu hṛdayāvadhi sasvanam ॥51॥

Closing the mouth properly, inhale through both the nostrils until the breath is felt from the throat to the heart, with a resonant sound. –51.

पूर्ववत्कुम्भयेत्प्राणं रेचयेदिडया तथा ।

श्लेष्मदोषहरं कण्ठे देहानलविवर्धनम् ॥५२॥

pūrvavatkumbhayetprāṇaṃ recayediḍayā tathā ।

śleṣmadoṣaharaṃ kaṇṭhe dehānalavivardhanam ॥52॥

Perform *kumbhaka* as before and exhale through the left nostril. This removes disorders of the throat caused by the *kapha* (phlegm), and stimulates the (digestive) fire in the body. –52.

नाडीजलोदराधातुगतदोषविनाशनम् ।

गच्छता तिष्ठता कार्यमुज्जाय्याख्यं तु कुम्भकम् ॥५३॥

nāḍījalodarādhātugatadoṣavināśanam ।

gacchatā tiṣṭhatā kāryamujjāyyākhyaṃ tu kumbhakam ॥53॥

Except for the *kumbhaka* part, this *prāṇāyāma* called *ujjāyī* can be practiced while sitting and walking. It destroys dropsy, diseases of the nāḍīs and imbalances of *dhātus* (humors). –53.

Practice of Sītkārī Prāṇāyāma

अथ सीत्कारी ।

सीत्कां कुर्यात्तथा वक्त्रे घ्राणेनैव विजृम्भिकाम् ।

एवमभ्यासयोगेन कामदेवो द्वितीयकः ॥५४॥

atha sītkārī ।

Now *sītkārī* is described.

sītkāṃ kuryāttathā vaktre ghrāṇenaiva vijṛmbhikām ।

evamabhyāsayogena kāmadevo dvitīyakaḥ ॥54॥

Draw the breath in through the mouth with a hissing sound, and then exhale through the nose, not by the mouth. By this practice of yoga, one becomes a second *kāmadeva* (the god of love). –54.

योगिनी चक्रसंमान्यः सृष्टिसंहारकारकः ।

न क्षुधा न तृषा निद्रा नैवालस्यं प्रजायते ॥५५॥

yoginī cakrasaṃmānyaḥ sṛṣṭisaṃhārakārakaḥ ।

na kṣudhā na tṛṣā nidrā naivālasyaṃ prajāyate ॥55॥

He is admired by the multitude of *yoginīs*. He becomes the creator and destroyer of the universe. He does not feel hunger, thirst, sleepiness or laziness. –55.

भवेत्सत्त्वं च देहस्य सर्वोपद्रववर्जितः ।

अनेन विधिना सत्यं योगीन्द्रो भूमिमण्डले ॥५६॥

bhavetsattvaṃ ca dehasya sarvopadravavarjitaḥ ।

anena vidhinā satyaṃ yogīndro bhūmimaṇḍale ॥56॥

By this practice, he gains strength of body and becomes free from all kinds of disasters. Truly, he becomes lord of the yogīs on this earth. –56.

Practice of Śītalī Prāṇāyāma

अथ शीतली ।

जिह्वया वायुमाकृष्य पूर्ववत्कुम्भसाधनम् ।

शनकैर्घ्राणरन्ध्राभ्यां रेचयेत्पवनं सुधीः ॥५७॥

atha śītalī ।

Now *śītalī* is described.

jihvayā vāyumākṛṣya pūrvavatkumbhasādhanam ।

śanakairghrāṇarandhrābhyāṃ recayetpavanaṃ sudhīḥ ॥57॥

Inhaling the breath through the tongue and performing *kumbhaka* as described earlier, the wise practitioner should slowly exhale the air through the nostrils. –57.

गुल्मप्लीहादिकान्रोगान्ज्वरं पित्तं क्षुधां तृषाम् ।

विषाणि शीतली नाम कुम्भिकेयं निहन्ति हि ॥५८॥

gulmaplīhādikān rogānjvaraṃ pittaṃ kṣudhāṃ tṛṣām ।

viṣāṇi śītalī nāma kumbhikeyaṃ nihanti hi ॥58॥

This *kumbhaka* called *śītalī* destroys enlargement of the spleen and other diseases like fever. It removes excesses of bile, thirst and hunger. It also eliminates the effects of poisons. –58.

Practice of Bhastrikā – Bellows Breath

अथ भस्त्रिका ।

ऊर्वोरुपरि संस्थाप्य शुभे पादतले उभे ।

पद्मासनं भवेदेतत्सर्वपापप्रणाशनम् ॥५९॥

atha bhastrikā ।

Now *bhastrikā* is described.

ūrvorupari saṃsthāpya śubhe pādatale ubhe ।

padmāsanaṃ bhavedetatsarvapāpapraṇāśanam ॥59॥

Place both feet on top of the opposite thighs. This is *padmāsana* that destroys all sins (diseases). –59.

सम्यक्पद्मासनं बद्ध्वा समग्रीवोदरः सुधीः ।

मुखं संयम्य यत्नेन प्राणं घ्राणेन रेचयेत् ॥६०॥

samyakpadmāsanaṃ baddhvā samagrīvodaram sudhīḥ ।

mukhaṃ saṃyamya yatnena prāṇaṃ ghrāṇena recayet ॥60॥

Sitting firmly in the *padmāsana*, the wise practitioner should keep his neck and abdomen upright. He should properly close the mouth and exhale *prāṇa* through his nostrils. –60.

यथा लगति हृत्कण्ठे कपालावधि सस्वनम् ।

वेगेन पूरयेच्चापि हृत्पद्मावधि मारुतम् ॥६१॥

yathā lagati hṛtkaṇṭhe kapālāvadhi sasvanam ।

vegena pūrayeccāpi hṛtpadmāvadhi mārutam ॥*61* ॥

Then the breath should quickly be inhaled up to the heart lotus with a sonorous sound that should be felt striking against the heart, throat and cranium (skull). –61.

पुनर्विरेचयेत्तद्वत्पूरयेच्च पुनः पुनः ।

यथैव लोहकारेण भस्त्रा वेगेन चाल्यते ॥६२॥

punarvirecayettadvatpūrayecca punaḥ punaḥ ।

yathaiva lohakāreṇa bhastrā vegena cālyate ॥*62* ॥

In this way the breath should be inhaled and exhaled again and again in an equal ratio (of inhalation and exhalation) like a black-smith rapidly moving his bellows. –62.

तथैव स्वशरीरस्थं चालयेत्पवनं धिया ।

यदा श्रमो भवेद्देहे तदा सूर्येण पूरयेत् ॥६३॥

tathaiva svaśarīrasthaṃ cālayetpavanaṃ dhiyā ।

yadā śramo bhaveddehe tadā sūryeṇa pūrayet ॥*63* ॥

In the same manner, one should keep the breath moving (by inhaling and exhaling) in the body. When the yogī feels tired, he should inhale through the right nostril. –63.

यथोदरं भवेत्पूर्णमनिलेन तथा लघु ।

धारयेन्नासिकां मध्यातर्जनीभ्यां विना दृढम् ॥६४॥

yathodaraṃ bhavetpūrṇamanilena tathā laghu ।

dhārayennāsikāṃ madhyātarjanībhyāṃ vinā dṛḍham ॥*64* ॥

When the abdomen is completely filled by air, then quickly hold the nostrils and *prāṇa* firmly, without using the index and middle fingers (i.e. by using the thumb, ring and little fingers). –64.

विधिवत्कुम्भकं कृत्वा रेचयेदिडयानिलम् ।

वातपित्तश्लेष्महरं शरीराग्निविवर्धनम् ॥६५॥

vidhivatkumbhakaṃ kṛtvā recayediḍayānilam ।

vātapittaśleṣmahāraṃ śarīrāgnivivardhanam ॥65॥

Having properly performed the *kumbhaka*, exhale through the left nostril. This removes the diseases arising from imbalances of wind, bile and phlegm or mucus and stimulates the digestive fire in the body. –65.

Bhastrikā Awakens the Kuṇḍalinī

कुण्डली बोधकं क्षिप्रं पवनं सुखदं हितम् ।

ब्रह्मनाडीमुखे संस्थकफाद्यर्गलनाशनम् ॥६६॥

kuṇḍalī bodhakaṃ kṣipraṃ pavanaṃ sukhadaṃ hitam ।

brahmanāḍīmukhe saṃsthakaphādyargalanāśanam ॥66॥

This *bhastrikā* quickly awakens the *kuṇḍalinī*. It is a pleasant and beneficial *prāṇāyāma*. It removes (the bolt।bar of) excess phlegm accumulated at the mouth of *brahma nāḍī* (*suṣumṇā*). –66.

सम्यग्गात्रसमुद्भूतग्रन्थित्रयविभेदकम् ।

विशेषेणैव कर्तव्यं भस्त्राख्यं कुम्भकं त्विदम् ॥६७॥

samyaggātrasamudbhūta granthitrayavibhedakam ।

viśeṣeṇaiva kartavyaṃ bhastrākhyaṃ kumbhakaṃ tvidām ॥67॥

Along with the awakening of the *kuṇḍalinī*, this *bhastrikā kumbhaka* enables the *prāṇa* to pierce through the three *granthis* (knots) generated in the body. So, it is one's duty to specially practice this *kumbhaka* called *bhastrikā*. –67.

Practice of Bhrāmarī - Bee Buzzing Prāṇāyāma

अथ भ्रामरी ।

वेगाद्घोषं पूरकं भृङ्गनादं भृङ्गीनादं रेचकं मन्दमन्दम् ।

योगीन्द्राणमेवमभ्यासयोगाच् चित्ते जाता काचिदानन्दलीला ॥६८॥

atha bhrāmarī ।

Now *bhrāmarī* is described.

vegādghoṣaṃ pūrakaṃ bhṛṅganādaṃ

bhṛṅgīnādaṃ rechakaṃ mandamandam ।

yogīndrāṇāmevamabhyāsayogāt

citte jātā kācidānandalīlā ॥68॥

Inhale quickly making the buzzing sound of a male black bee, and exhale quite slowly making the soft buzzing sound of a female black bee. Through the constant practice of this yoga, the mind of the great yogī merges into supreme bliss. –68.

Practice of Mūrcchā or Fainting Prāṇāyāma

अथ मूर्च्छा ।

पूरकान्ते गाढतरं बद्ध्वा जालन्धरं शनैः ।

रेचयेन्मूर्च्छाख्येयं मनोमूर्च्छा सुखप्रदा ॥६९॥

atha mūrcchā ।

Now *mūrcchā* is described.

pūrakānte gāḍhataraṃ baddhvā jālandharaṃ śanaiḥ ।

recayenmūrcchanākhyeyaṃ manomūrcchā sukhapradā ॥69॥

At the end of inhalation, perform an intensely stable *jālandhara bandha*. Then exhale slowly. This is called *mūrcchā* or fainting *prāṇāyāma*. It induces an inactive state of mind and gives pleasure. –69.

Practice of Plāvinī – Gulping Prāṇāyāma

अथ प्लाविनी ।

अन्तः प्रवर्तितोदारमारुतापूरितोदरः ।

पयस्यगाधेऽपि सुखात्प्लवते पद्मपत्रवत् ॥७०॥

atha plāvinī ।

Now *plāvinī* is described.

antaḥ pravartitodāramārutāpūritodaraḥ ।

payasyagādhe'pi sukhātplavate padmapatravat ॥70॥

When the inner abdomen is largely distended, being filled with air, one can pleasantly float on shallow water like a leaf of a lotus. –70.

Types of Prāṇāyāma and Kumbhaka

प्राणायामस्त्रिधा प्रोक्तो रेचपूरककुम्भकैः ।

सहितः केवलश्चेति कुम्भको द्विविधो मतः ॥७१॥

prāṇāyāmastridhā prokto recakapūrakakumbhakaiḥ ।

sahitaḥ kevalaśceti kumbhako dvividho mataḥ ॥71॥

It is said that there are three kinds of *prāṇāyāma*: *rechaka* (exhalation), *pūraka* (inhalation) and *kumbhaka* (retention). *Kumbhaka* is of two kinds: *sahita* (retention of breath with controlled inhalation and exhalation) and *kevala* (spontaneous retention of breath). –71.

यावत्केवलसिद्धिः स्यात्सहितं तावदभ्यसेत् ।

रेचकं पूरकं मुक्त्वा सुखं यद्वायुधारणम् ॥७२॥

yāvatkevalasiddhiḥ syātsahitaṃ tāvadabhyaset ।

recakaṃ pūrakaṃ muktvā sukhaṃ yadvāyudhāraṇam ॥72॥

Until perfection is attained in *kevala kumbhaka, sahita kumbhaka* should be practiced. Being freed from inhalation and exhalation, retention of the *prāṇa* becomes pleasant. –72.

प्राणायामोऽयमित्युक्तः स वै केवलकुम्भकः ।

कुम्भके केवले सिद्धे रेचपूरकवर्जिते ॥७३॥

prāṇāyāmo'yamityuktaḥ sa vai kevalakumbhakaḥ ।

kumbhake kevale siddhe recakapūrakavarjite ॥73॥

This *prāṇāyāma* of achieving mastery over the (complete) retention of the *prāṇa*, without inhalation and exhalation, is certainly called *kevala kumbhaka*. –73.

Benefit of Kevala Kumbhaka

न तस्य दुर्लभं किंचित्त्रिषु लोकेषु विद्यते ।

शक्तः केवलकुम्भेन यथेष्टं वायुधारणात् ॥७४॥

na tasya durlabhaṃ kiñcittriṣu lokeṣu vidyate ।

śaktaḥ kevalakumbhena yatheṣṭaṃ vāyudhāraṇāt ॥74॥

For one who has gained the power of retaining the *prāṇa* through (the practice of) *kevala kumbhaka*, there is nothing unattainable by him in the three worlds. –74.

Kevala Kumbhaka Accomplishes Rāja Yoga

राजयोगपदं चापि लभते नात्र संशयः ।

कुम्भकात्कुण्डलीबोधः कुण्डलीबोधतो भवेत् ।

अनर्गला सुषुम्णा च हठसिद्धिश्च जायते ॥७५॥

rājayogapadaṃ cāpi labhate nātra saṃśayaḥ ।

kumbhakātkuṇḍalībodhaḥ kuṇḍalībodhato bhavet ।

anargalā suṣumṇā ca haṭhasiddhiśca jāyate ॥75॥

There is no doubt that *kevala kumbhaka* also achieves the state of *Rāja Yoga*. Through *kumbhaka*, *kuṇḍalinī* is awakened. By its awakening it becomes the opener (of the *suṣumṇā*). *Suṣumṇā* becomes unlocked (free of obstruction) and perfection in *Haṭha Yoga* is attained. –75.

Haṭha Yoga and Rāja Yoga Support One Another

हठं विना राजयोगो राजयोगं विना हठः ।

न सिध्यति ततो युग्ममानिष्पत्तेः समभ्यसेत् ॥७६॥

haṭhaṃ vinā rājayogo rājayogaṃ vinā haṭhaḥ ।

na sidhyati tato yugmamāniṣpatteḥ samabhyaset ॥76॥

Perfection cannot be attained in *Rāja Yo*ga without *Haṭha Y*oga. Similarly, *Haṭha Yoga* cannot be accomplished without *Rāja Yoga*. Therefore, one should properly practice both (*Haṭha Yoga* and *Rāja Yoga*) until he attains perfection (in *Rāja Yoga*). –76.

कुम्भकप्राणरोधान्ते कुर्याच्चित्तं निराश्रयम् ।

एवमभ्यासयोगेन राजयोगपदं व्रजेत् ॥७७॥

kumbhakaprāṇarodhānte kuryāccittaṃ nirāśrayam ।

evamabhyāsayogena rājayogapadaṃ vrajet ॥77॥

At the end of the retention of *prāṇa*, the mind should be made *nirāśraya* (literally, without support), which is free from any mental modifications. In this way, by constant practice of yoga, one is raised to the highest state of *Rāja Yoga*. –77.

Signs of Perfection in Haṭha Yoga

वपुः कृशत्वं वदने प्रसन्नता नादस्फुटत्वं नयने सुनिर्मले ।

अरोगता बिन्दुजयोऽग्निदीपनं नाडीविशुद्धिर्हठसिद्धिलक्षणम् ॥७८॥

vapuḥ kṛśatvaṃ vadane prasannatā

nādasphuṭatvaṃ nayane sunirmale ।

arogatā bindujayo'gnidīpanaṃ

nāḍīviśuddhirhaṭhasiddhilakṣaṇam ॥78॥

These are the signs of perfection in (the practice of) *Haṭha Yoga*: slender body, pleasing face and speech, hearing of inner sounds, bright and clean eyes, freedom from diseases, control of the *bindu* (seminal fluid), strong digestive fire and purification of all the *nāḍīs*. –78.

इति हठयोगप्रदीपिकायां द्वितीयोपदेशः ॥

iti haṭhayogapradīpikāyāṃ dvitīyopadeśaḥ ॥

Thus ends the Chapter Two of *Haṭha Yoga Pradīpikā.*

CHAPTER THREE

तृतीयोपदेशः

Discourse on Mudrā

Kuṇḍalinī is the Support of Yoga and Tantra

सशैलवनधात्रीणां यथाधारोऽहिनायकः ।

सर्वेषां योगतन्त्राणां तथाधारो हि कुण्डली ॥१॥

saśailavanadhātrīṇāṃ yathādhāro'hināyakaḥ ।

sarveṣāṃ yogatantrāṇāṃ tathādhāro hi kuṇḍalī ॥1॥

As *Ahināyaka* (the lord of the serpents, who is also called *Vāsukī*) supports this whole universe along with its mountains and forests, so *Kuṇḍalinī* is the support of all the yoga practices. –1.

सुप्ता गुरुप्रसादेन यदा जागर्ति कुण्डली ।

तदा सर्वाणि पद्मानि भिद्यन्ते ग्रन्थयोऽपि च ॥२॥

suptā guruprasādena yadā jāgarti kuṇḍalī ।

tadā sarvāṇi padmāni bhidyante granthayo'pi ca ॥2॥

When the sleeping *Kuṇḍalinī* is awakened by the grace of the guru, then all the *padmas* (lotuses /*cakras*) and *granthis* (the knots) are pierced through. –2.

प्राणस्य शून्यपदवी तदा राजपथायते ।

तदा चित्तं निरालम्बं तदा कालस्य वञ्चनम् ॥३॥

prāṇasya śūnyapadavī tathā rājapathāyate ।

tadā cittaṃ nirālambaṃ tadā kālasya vañcanam ॥3॥

Then *prāṇa* gets into the state of void (emptiness) and *suṣumṇā* becomes the highway for *prāṇa*. Then the mind becomes supportless (i.e. free from its thoughts and modifications) and death is deceived. –3.

Various Names of Suṣumṇā

सुषुम्णा शून्यपदवी ब्रह्मरन्ध्रः महापथः ।

श्मशानं शाम्भवी मध्यमार्गश्चेत्येकवाचकाः ॥४॥

suṣumṇā śūnyapadavī brahmarandhram mahāpathaḥ ।

śmaśānaṃ śāmbhavī madhyamārgaścetyekavācakāḥ ॥4॥

Suṣumṇā, *śūnyapadavī* (the state of void), *brahmarandhra* (the way|hole to *Brahman*), *mahāpatha* (the highway), *śmaśāna* (the burning ground), *śāmbhavī* (belonging to *Śiva*) and *madhyamārga* (the middle path), all these are said to be one and the same thing. –4.

तस्मात्सर्वप्रयत्नेन प्रबोधयितुमीश्वरीम् ।

ब्रह्मद्वारमुखे सुप्तां मुद्राभ्यासं समाचरेत् ॥५॥

tasmātsarvaprayatnena prabodhayitumīśvarīm ।

brahmadvāramukhe suptāṃ mudrābhyāsaṃ samācaret ॥5॥

So, the goddess sleeping at the doorway to *Brahma* (the Absolute) should be aroused with utmost effort through the practice of *mudrās*. –5.

Types of Mudrās and Bandhas

महामुद्रा महाबन्धो महावेधश्च खेचरी ।

उड्डीयानं मूलबन्धश्च बन्धो जालन्धराभिधः ॥६॥

करणी विपरीताख्या वज्रोली शक्तिचालनम् ।

इदं हि मुद्रादशकं जरामरणनाशनम् ॥७॥

mahāmudrā mahābandho mahāvedhaśca khecarī ।

uḍḍyānaṃ mūlabandhaśca bandho jālandharābhidhaḥ ॥6॥

karaṇī viparītākhyā vajrolī śakticālanam ।

idāṃ hi mudrādaśakaṃ jarāmaraṇanāśanam ॥7॥

Mahā mudrā, mahā bandha, mahā vedha, khecarī, uḍḍiyāna, mūla bandha, jālandhara bandha, viparīta karaṇī, vajrolī and *śakti cālana* are the ten *mudrās* that destroy old age and death. –6-7.

आदिनाथोदितं दिव्यमष्टैश्वर्यप्रदायकम् ।

वल्लभं सर्वसिद्धानां दुर्लभं मरुतामपि ॥८॥

ādināthoditaṃ divyamaṣṭaiśvaryapradāyakam ।

vallabhaṃ sarvasiddhānāṃ durlabhaṃ marutāmapi ॥8॥

These *mudrās* were told by the primeval Lord *Śiva*. They give the eight divine powers. These powers are desired by all *siddhas*, and they are difficult to attain even by gods. –8.

गोपनीयं प्रयत्नेन यथा रत्नकरण्डकम् ।

कस्यचिन्नैव वक्तव्यं कुलस्त्रीसुरतं यथा ॥९॥

gopanīyaṃ prayatnena yathā ratnakaraṇḍakam ।

kasyacinnaiva vaktavyaṃ kulastrīsurataṃ yathā ॥9॥

These *mudrās* should be carefully kept secret like a box of precious jewels. It should not be told to anyone, similar to sexual relations with a woman of noble family. –9.

Practice of Mahā Mudrā

अथ महामुद्रा ।

पादमूलेन वामेन योनिं सम्पीड्य दक्षिणाम् ।

प्रसारितं पदं कृत्वा कराभ्यां धारयेद्दृढम् ॥१०॥

atha mahāmudrā ।

Now *mahā mudrā* is described.

pādamūlena vāmena yoniṃ sampīḍya dakṣiṇām ।

prasāritaṃ padaṃ kṛtvā karābhyāṃ dhārayeddṛḍham ॥10॥

While pressing the perineum with the left heel, stretch out the right leg. Firmly take hold of the right foot with the hands. –10.

कण्ठे बन्धं समारोप्य धारयेद्वायुमूर्ध्वतः ।

यथा दण्डहतः सर्पो दण्डाकारः प्रजायते ॥११॥

kaṇṭhe bandhaṃ samāropya dhārayedvāyumūrdhvataḥ ।

yathā daṇḍahataḥ sarpo daṇḍākāraḥ prajāyate ॥11॥

By properly fixing the *bandha* (lock) in the throat (*jālandhara bandha*), retain the *vāyu* (breath) upwards; the *prāṇa* raises upright, just like a snake beaten by a stick becomes straight. -11.

ऋज्वीभूता तथा शक्तिः कुण्डली सहसा भवेत् ।

तदा सा मरणावस्था जायते द्विपुटाश्रया ॥१२॥

ṛjvībhūtā tathā śaktiḥ kuṇḍalī sahasā bhavet ।

tadā sā maraṇāvasthā jāyate dvipuṭāśrayā ॥12॥

Then the *kuṇḍalinī śakti* becomes straight at once. The two *nāḍīs* (*idā* and *piṅgalā*) become dead as the *prāṇa* leaves them (i.e. enters *suṣumṇā*). –12.

ततः शनैः शनैरेव रेचयेन्नैव वेगतः ।

इयं खलु महामुद्रा महासिद्धैः प्रदर्शिता ॥१३॥

tataḥ śanaiḥ śanaireva recayennaiva vegataḥ ।

iyaṃ khalu mahāmudrā mahāsiddhaiḥ pradarśitā ॥13॥

Then exhale very slowly and not forcibly. This is verily *mahā mudrā*, described by the great *siddhas*. –13.

महाक्लेशादयो दोषाः क्षीयन्ते मरणादयः ।

महामुद्रां च तेनैव वदन्ति विबुधोत्तमाः ॥१४॥

mahākleśādayo doṣāḥ kṣīyante maraṇādayaḥ ।

mahāmudrāṃ ca tenaiva vadanti vibudhottamāḥ ॥14॥

Mahā mudrā destroys *mahākleśas* (the great afflictions) and the causes of death. This is why it is called 'the great *mudrā*' by the excellent wise men. –14.

चन्द्राङ्गे तु समभ्यस्य सूर्याङ्गे पुनरभ्यसेत् ।

यावत्तुल्या भवेत्सङ्ख्या ततो मुद्रां विसर्जयेत् ॥१५॥

candrāṅge ca samabhyasya sūryāṅge punarabhyaset ।

yāvattūlyā bhavetsaṅkhyā tato mudrāṃ visarjayet ॥15॥

After first practicing on the left side, practice on the right side. When the number of rounds is equal on both sides, then finish the practice of the *mudrā*. –15.

न हि पथ्यमपथ्यं वा रसाः सर्वेऽपि नीरसाः ।

अपि भुक्तं विषं घोरं पीयूषमपि जीर्यति ॥१६॥

na hi pathyamapathyaṃ vā rasāḥ sarve'pi nīrasāḥ ।

api bhuktaṃ viṣaṃ ghoraṃ pīyūṣamapi jīryati ॥*16*॥

There is nothing wholesome or unwholesome for the practitioner of this *mudrā*. All edibles, with good taste or without any taste, are equally digested. Even horrible poison is assimilated like nectar. –16.

क्षयकुष्ठगुदावर्तगुल्माजीर्णपुरोगमाः ।

तस्य दोषाः क्षयं यान्ति महामुद्रां तु योऽभ्यसेत् ॥१७॥

kṣayakuṣṭhagudāvartagulmājīrṇapurogamāḥ ।

tasya doṣāḥ kṣayaṃ yānti mahāmudrāṃ tu yo'bhyaset ॥*17*॥

Mahā mudrā eliminates consumption, leprosy, piles, constipation and all the major disorders. He who practices *mahā mudrā*, all his diseases are certainly destroyed. –17.

कथितेयं महामुद्रा महासिद्धिकरा नृणाम् ।

गोपनीया प्रयत्नेन न देया यस्य कस्यचित् ॥१८॥

kathiteyaṃ mahāmudrā mahāsiddhikarā nṛṇām ।

gopanīyā prayatnena na deyā yasyakasyacit ॥*18*॥

Thus this *mahā mudrā*, the giver of great perfections to men, has been described. This should be kept carefully secret, and should not be given to everyone. –18.

Practice of Mahābandha

अथ महाबन्धः ।

पार्ष्णिं वामस्य पादस्य योनिस्थाने नियोजयेत् ।

वामोरुपरि संस्थाप्य दक्षिणं चरणं तथा ॥१९॥

atha mahābandhaḥ ।

Now *mahā bandha* is described.

pārṣṇiṃ vāmasya pādasya yonisthāne niyojayet ।

vāmorūpari saṃsthāpya dakṣiṇaṃ caraṇaṃ tathā ॥19॥

Press the perineum with the left heel and place the right foot upon the left thigh. –19.

पूरयित्वा ततो वायुं हृदये चुबुकं दृढम् ।

निष्पीड्यं वायुमाकुञ्च्य मनोमध्ये नियोजयेत् ॥२०॥

pūrayitvā tato vāyuṃ hṛdaye cibukaṃ dṛḍham ।

niṣpīḍya vāyumākuñcya manomadhye niyojayet ॥20॥

Having inhaled the breath, place the chin firmly against the chest (perform *jālandhara bandha*), contract the perineum, and concentrate on the *suṣumṇā nāḍī*. –20.

धारयित्वा यथाशक्ति रेचयेदनिलं शनैः ।

सव्याङ्गे तु समभ्यस्य दक्षाङ्गे पुनरभ्यसेत् ॥२१॥

dhārayitvā yathāśakti recayedanilaṃ śanaiḥ ।

savyāṅge tu samabhyasya dakṣāṅge punarabhyaset ॥21॥

Having retained the breath as long as possible, exhale slowly. After properly completing the practice on the left side, practice again on the right side. –21.

मतमत्र तु केषांचित्कण्ठबन्धं विवर्जयेत् ।

राजदन्तस्थजिह्वाया बन्धः शस्तो भवेदिति ॥२२॥

matamatra tu keṣāñcitkaṇṭhabandhaṃ vivarjayet ।

rājadantasthajihvāyāṃ bandhaḥ śasto bhaveditі ॥22॥

Some have the opinion that the throat lock should be abandoned, and that it is excellent to press the tongue firmly against the front teeth. –22.

अयं तु सर्वनाडीनामूर्ध्वं गतिनिरोधकः ।

अयं खलु महाबन्धो महासिद्धिप्रदायकः ॥२३॥

ayaṃ tu sarvanāḍīnāmūrdhvaṃ gatinirodhakaḥ ।

ayaṃ khalu mahābandho mahāsiddhipradāyakaḥ ॥23॥

This (pressing the tongue against the front teeth during *mahā bandha*) stops the upward flow of *prāṇa* through all the *nāḍīs*. Indeed, this is *mahā bandha*, the contributor of great *siddhis*. –23.

कालपाशमहाबन्धविमोचनविचक्षणः ।

त्रिवेणीसङ्गमं धत्ते केदारं प्रापयेन्मनः ॥२४॥

kālapāśamahābandhavimocanavicakṣaṇaḥ ।

triveñīsaṅgamaṃ dhatte kedāraṃ prāpayenmanaḥ ॥24॥

This frees the wise practitioner from the great noose of death, and brings about the union of the three *nāḍīs* (*iḍā*, *piṅgalā* and *suṣumṇā*). It enables the mind to reach *kedāra* (the seat of *Śiva*, i.e., *ajñā cakra*). –24.

रूपलावण्यसम्पन्ना यथा स्त्री पुरुषं विना ।

महामुद्रामहाबन्धौ निष्फलौ वेधवर्जितौ ॥२५॥

rūpalāvaṇyasampannā yathā strī puruṣaṃ vinā ।

mahāmudrāmahābandhau niṣphalau vedhavarjitau ॥25॥

Just as a very beautiful woman is fruitless without a husband, so *mahā mudrā* and *mahā bandha* become unfruitful without *mahā vedha*. –25.

Practice of Mahāvedha

अथ महावेधः ।

महाबन्धस्थितो योगी कृत्वा पूरकमेकधीः ।

वायूनां गतिमावृत्य निभृतं कण्ठमुद्रया ॥२६॥

atha mahāvedhaḥ ।

Now *mahā vedha* is described.

mahābandhasthito yogī kṛtvā pūrakamekadhīḥ ।

vāyūnāṃ gatimāvṛtya nibhṛtaṃ kaṇṭhamudrāyā ॥26॥

The yogī, seated in the position of *mahā bandha*, should inhale with a concentrated mind and stop the movement of *prāṇa* by performing the *jālandhara bandha.* –26.

समहस्तयुगो भूमौ स्फिचौ सनाडयेच्छनैः ।
पुटद्वयमतिक्रम्य वायुः स्फुरति मध्यगः ॥२७॥

samahāstayugo bhūmau sphicau santāḍayecchanaiḥ ।
puṭadvayamatikramya vāyuḥ sphurati madhyagaḥ ॥27॥

Placing the palms flat on the ground, the yogī should bounce the buttocks gently against the ground. By this the *prāṇa* goes beyond the two *nāḍīs* (*idā* and *piṅgalā*) and enters tremulously into the middle (*suṣumṇā nāḍī*). –27.

सोमसूर्याग्निसम्बन्धो जायते चामृताय वै ।
मृतावस्था समुत्पन्ना ततो वायुं विरेचयेत् ॥२८॥

somasūryāgnisambandho jāyate cāmṛtāya vai ।
mṛtāvasthā samutpannā tato vāyuṃ virecayet ॥28॥

Then the union of *soma, sūrya* and *agni* (the moon, the sun and fire – *idā, piṅgalā* and *suṣumṇā*) takes place. It certainly leads to immortality. When a death like state occurs (in the body), then the breath should be exhaled. –28.

महावेधोऽयमभ्यासान्महासिद्धिप्रदायकः ।
वलीपलितवेपघ्नः सेव्यते साधकोत्तमैः ॥२९॥

mahāvedho'yamabhyāsānmahāsiddhipradāyakaḥ ।
valīpalitavepaghnaḥ sevyate sādhakottamaiḥ ॥29॥

This is *mahā vedha*, and gives great perfections through its practice. It removes wrinkles, grey hairs and trembling. So, it is served (performed) by the excellent practitioners. –29.

एतत्त्रयं महागुह्यं जरामृत्युविनाशनम् ।
वह्निवृद्धिकरं चैव ह्यणिमादिगुणप्रदम् ॥३०॥

etattrayaṃ mahāguhyaṃ jarāmṛtyuvināśanam ।
vahnivṛddhikaraṃ caiva hyaṇimādiguṇapradam ॥30॥

These three *bandhas* are great secrets that destroy old age and death, stimulate the digestive fire and confer the *siddhis* (perfections) like *aṇimā* and others. –30.

अष्टधा क्रियते चैव यामे यामे दिने दिने ।

पुण्यसम्भारसन्धाय पापौघभिदुरं सदा ।

सम्यक्शिक्षावतामेवं स्वल्पं प्रथमसाधनम् ॥३१॥

aṣṭadhā kriyate caiva yāme yāme dine dine ।

puṇyasaṃbhārasandhāyi pāpaughabhiduraṃ sadā ।

samyakṣikṣāvatāmevaṃ svalpaṃ prathamasādhanam ॥31॥

They should be practiced eight times daily at every *yama* (each period of three hours). They always increase virtues and remove multitude of sin. Those who are properly instructed (by the guru) should perform them little by little at first. –31.

Practice of Khecarī Mudrā

अथ खेचरी ।

कपालकुहरे जिह्वा प्रविष्टा विपरीतगा ।

भ्रुवोरन्तर्गता दृष्टिर्मुद्रा भवति खेचरी ॥३२॥

atha khecarī ।

Now *khecarī* is described.

kapālakuhare jihvā praviṣṭā viparītagā ।

bhruvorantargatā dṛṣṭirmudrā bhavati khecarī ॥32॥

Turn the tongue backwards and enter it into the cavity of the skull. Fix the gaze between the eyebrows. This is *khecarī mudrā*. –32.

छेदनचालनदोहैः कलां क्रमेणाथ वर्धयेत्तावत् ।

सा यावद्भ्रूमध्यं स्पृशति तदा खेचरीसिद्धिः ॥३३॥

chedanacālanadohaiḥ kalāṃ krameṇa vardhayettāvat ।

sā yāvad bhrūmadhyaṃsmṛśati tadā khecarīsiddhiḥ ॥33॥

Through the practical art of cutting, shaking and milking the tongue, it should be elongated until it touches the middle of the eyebrows. Then *khecarī mudrā* is perfected. –33.

स्नुहीपत्रनिभं शस्त्रं सुतीक्ष्णं स्निग्धनिर्मलम् ।
समादाय ततस्तेन रोममात्रं समुच्छिनेत् ॥३४॥

snuhīpatranibhaṃ śastraṃ sutīkṣṇaṃ snigdhanirmalam ।
samādāya tatastena romamātraṃ samucchinet ॥34॥

Take a clean knife or a razor as sharp as the leaf of the milk-hedge plant, and cut the membrane under the tongue (fraenum lingum) by a hair's breadth. –34.

ततः सैन्धवपथ्याभ्यां चूर्णिताभ्यां प्रघर्षयेत् ।
पुनः सप्तदिने प्राप्ते रोममात्रं समुच्छिनेत् ॥३५॥

tataḥ saindhavapathyābhyāṃ cūrṇitābhyāṃ pragharṣayet ।
punaḥ saptadine prāpte romamātraṃ samucchinet ॥35॥

Then rub the cut area with a compound of powdered rock salt and *pathyā* (*haritaki* – the fruit of yellow myrobalane). After seven days, cut it again by a hair's breadth. –35.

एवं क्रमेण षण्मासं नित्यं युक्तः समाचरेत् ।
षण्मासाद्रसनामूलशिराबन्धः प्रणश्यति ॥३६॥

evaṃ krameṇa ṣaṇmāsaṃ nityaṃ yuktaḥ samācaret ।
ṣaṇmāsādrasanāmūlaśirābandhaḥ praṇaśyati ॥36॥

In this way, the practice should be continued properly for six months. After six months, the membrane (fraenum lingum) connecting the base of the tongue is cut off. –36.

कलां पराङ्मुखीं कृत्वा त्रिपथे परियोजयेत् ।
सा भवेत्खेचरी मुद्रा व्योमचक्रं तदुच्यते ॥३७॥

kalāṃ parāṅmukhīṃ kṛtvā tripathe pariyojayet ।
sā bhavetkhecarī mudrā vyomacakraṃ taducyate ॥37॥

Having turned the tongue upwards, fix it on the *tripatha* (literally, the three ways, i.e. junction of the three organs – oesophagus, windpipe and palate). This is *khecarī mudrā*. It is called *vyomacakra* (the center of the ether). –37.

रसनामूर्ध्वगां कृत्वा क्षणार्धमपि तिष्ठति ।
विषैर्विमुच्यते योगी व्याधिमृत्युजरादिभिः ॥३८॥

rasanāmūrdhvagāṃ kṛtvā kṣaṇārdhamapi tiṣṭhati ।
viṣairvimucyate yogī vyādhimṛtyujarādibhiḥ ॥38॥

The yogī who remains with his tongue turned upwards even for half a moment, he is freed from poisons, disease, old age and death. –38.

न रोगो मरणं तन्द्रा न निद्रा न क्षुधा तृषा ।
न च मूर्च्छा भवेत्तस्य यो मुद्रां वेत्ति खेचरीम् ॥३९॥

na rogo maraṇaṃ tandrā na nidrā na kṣudhā tṛṣā ।
na ca mūrcchā bhavettasya yo mudrāṃ vetti khecarīm ॥39॥

He who knows *khecarī mudrā*, he does not suffer from disease, death, laziness, sleep, hunger, thirst or ignorance. –39.

पीड्यते न स रोगेण लिप्यते न च कर्मणा ।
बाध्यते न स कालेन यो मुद्रां वेत्ति खेचरीम् ॥४०॥

pīḍyate na sa rogeṇa lipyate na ca karmaṇā ।
bādhyate na sa kālena yo mudrāṃ vetti khecarīm ॥40॥

He who knows *khecarī mudrā* is not afflicted by any disease. He is not affected by any karma. He is not bound by time (death). –40.

चित्तं चरति खे यस्माज्जिह्वा चरति खे गता ।
तेनैषा खेचरी नाम मुद्रा सिद्धैर्निरूपिता ॥४१॥

cittaṃ carati khe yasmājjihvā carati khe gatā ।
tenaiṣā khecarī nāma mudrā siddhairnirūpitā ॥41॥

The mind moves in the *Brahman* because the tongue moves in that space (entering the cavity above the palate). Therefore, the perfected ones have named this *mudrā khecarī* (*mudrā* that helps one move to Brahman). –41.

खेचर्या मुद्रितं येन विवरं लम्बिकोर्ध्वतः ।
न तस्य क्षरते बिन्दुः कामिन्याः श्लेषितस्य च ॥४२॥

khecaryā mudritaṃ yena vivaraṃ lambikordhvataḥ ।

na tasya kṣarate binduḥ kāminyāḥ śleṣitasya ca ॥42॥

When the practitioner closes the cavity (at the upper part) of the palate by *khecarī mudrā* with his tongue upwards, his seminal fluid is not emitted even when a young amorous woman embraces him. –42.

चलितोऽपि यदा बिन्दुः सम्प्राप्तो योनिमण्डलम् ।

व्रजत्यूर्ध्वं हृतः शक्त्या निबद्धो योनिमुद्रया ॥४३॥

calito'pi yadā binduḥ samprāpto yonimaṇḍalam ।

vrājatyūrdhvaṃ hṛtaḥ śaktyā nibaddho yonimudrāyā ॥43॥

Even when the seminal fluid has moved down to the genital organ, it is captured by the force of the practice of *yoni mudrā* and taken back up to its place. –43.

ऊर्ध्वजिह्वः स्थिरो भूत्वा सोमपानं करोति यः ।

मासार्धेन न सन्देहो मृत्युं जयति योगवित् ॥४४॥

ūrdhvajihvaḥ sthiro bhūtvā somapānaṃ karoti yaḥ ।

māsārdhena na sandeho mṛtyuṃ jayati yogavit ॥44॥

The wise yogī who drinks the fluid of the moon with tongue turned upwards, keeping a stable body and steady mind, certainly conquers death within fifteen days. –44.

नित्यं सोमकलापूर्णं शरीरं यस्य योगिनः ।

तक्षकेणापि दष्टस्य विषं तस्य न सर्पति ॥४५॥

nityaṃ somakalāpūrṇaṃ śarīre yasya yoginaḥ ।

takṣakeṇāpi daṣṭasya viṣaṃ tasya na sarpati ॥45॥

The yogī whose body is always full of the moon's nectar, even if he is bitten by the king of snakes *Takṣaka*, the poison does not pass through his body. –45.

इन्धनानि यथा वह्निस्तैलवर्ति च दीपकः ।

तथा सोमकलापूर्णं देही देहं न मुञ्चति ॥४६॥

indhanāni yathā vahnistailavartiṃ ca dīpakaḥ ।

tathā somakalāpūrṇaṃ dehī dehaṃ na muñcati ॥46॥

So long as there is fuel, the fire does not go out. So long as there is oil and wick in the lamp, the light does not die out. Similarly, so long as the body is full of the moon's nectar, *Dehi* (the indweller i.e. the Individual Self) does not leave the body. –46.

गोमांसं भक्षयेन्नित्यं पिबेदमरवारुणीम् ।

कुलीनं तमहं मन्ये चेतरे कुलघातकाः ॥४७॥

gomāṃsaṃ bhakṣayennityaṃ pibedamaravāruṇīm ।

kulīnaṃ tamahāṃ manye cetare kulaghātakāḥ ॥47॥

He who eats *gomāṃsa* (literally, the flesh of a cow) daily and drinks *amaravāruṇī* (the wine of immortality), I consider him of highly noble family. Others are *kulaghātaka* (the destroyers of their parentage). –47.

गोशब्देनोदिता जिह्वा तत्प्रवेशो हि तालुनि ।

गोमांसभक्षणं तत्तु महापातकनाशनम् ॥४८॥

gośabdenoditā jihvā tatpraveśo hi tāluni ।

gomāṃsabhakṣaṇaṃ tattu mahāpātakanāśanam ॥48॥

The word "*go*" means tongue. When it is entered into the cavity of the upper palate, this is "eating the flesh of the cow". This destroys the five great sins. –48.

जिह्वाप्रवेशसम्भूतवह्निनोत्पादितः खलु ।

चन्द्रात्स्रवति यः सारः सा स्यादमरवारुणी ॥४९॥

jihvāpraveśasambhūtavahninotpāditaḥ khalu ।

candrātsravati yaḥ sāraḥ sā syādamaravāruṇī ॥49॥

Verily, the tongue entering the cavity produces heat. It causes the flow of the essence (nectar) from the moon that is called *amaravāruṇī* (literally, immortal wine). –49.

चुम्बन्ती यदि लम्बिकाग्रमनिशं जिह्वारसस्यन्दिनी

सक्षारा कटुकाम्लदुग्धसदृशी मध्वाज्यतुल्या तथा ।

व्याधीनां हरणं जरान्तकरणं शस्त्रागमोदीरणं

तस्य स्यादमरत्वमष्टगुणितं सिद्धाङ्गनाकर्षणम् ॥५०॥

cumbantī yadi lambikāgramaniśaṃ jihvārasaspandinī

sakṣārā kaṭukāmladugdhasadṛśī madhvājyatulyā tathā ।

vyādhīnāṃ haraṇaṃ jarāntakaraṇaṃ śastrāgamodīraṇaṃ

tasya syādamaratvamaṣṭaguṇitaṃ siddhāṅganākarṣaṇam ॥50॥

If the tip of the tongue constantly presses the cavity, the nectar exuding from the moon tastes salty, pungent and acidic. It is also similar to milk, honey and ghee in taste. It eliminates all diseases, and prevents old age and weapons of all kinds. It confers the ability to speak about all *vedic* knowledge. This act of *khecarī* confers the practitioner immortality, the eight *siddhis* (supernatural powers) and the power to attract the *siddhas* and beautiful women. –50.

मूर्ध्नः षोडशपत्रपद्मगलितं प्राणादवाप्तं हठाद्

ऊर्द्व्हास्यो रसनां नियम्य विवरे शक्तिं परां चिन्तयन् ।

उत्कल्लोलकलाजलं च विमलं धारामयं यः पिबेन्

निर्व्याधिः स मृणालकोमलवपुर्योगी चिरं जीवति ॥५१॥

mūrdhnaḥ ṣoḍashapatrapadmagalitaṃ prāṇādavāptaṃ haṭhād

ūrdvhāsyo rasanāṃ niyamya vivare śaktiṃ parāṃ cintayan ।

utkallolakalājalaṃ ca vimalaṃ dhārāmayaṃ yaḥ piben

nirvyādhiḥ sa mṛṇālakomalavapuryohī ciraṃ jīvati ॥51॥

He who first closes the cavity of the palate with the tongue curved upwards, contemplates the supreme power (*Parāśakti* i.e. *Kuṇḍalinī*) and then drinks the clean stream of nectar dripping from the moon in the head into the sixteen-petaled lotus (*viśuddhi cakra* in the throat), gained by means of control of the *prāṇa* through the practice of *Haṭha Yoga*, is a yogī freed from all diseases, and lives long with a body soft and beautiful as the stem of a lotus. –51.

यत्प्रालेयं प्रहितसुषिरं मेरुमूर्धान्तरस्थं

तस्मिंस्तत्त्वं प्रवदति सुधीस्तन्मुखं निम्नगानाम् ।
चन्द्रात्सारः स्रवति वपुषस्तेन मृत्युर्नराणां
तद्बध्नीयात्सुकरणमधो नान्यथा कायसिद्धिः ॥५२॥

yatprāleyaṃ prahitasuṣiraṃ merumūrdhāntarasthaṃ
tasmiṃstattvaṃ pravadati sudhīstanmukhaṃ nimnagānām ।
candrātsāraḥ sravati vapuṣastena mṛtyurnarāṇāṃ
tadbadhnīyātsukaraṇamadho nānyathā kāyasiddhiḥ ॥52॥

From the top interior part of the *meru* (*suṣumṇā*) in the cavity, the nectar is secreted. The wise with pure intellect say there is the *Ātmā* (Universal Self) within it. It is the source of the descending *nāḍīs – iḍā, piṅgalā* and *suṣumṇā*. The nectar, which is the essence of the body, flows out from the moon and thus causes the death of human beings. So, it (the nectar) should be stopped from flowing out. This (*khecarī mudrā*) is an excellent means of practice. There is no other means of achieving *kāyā siddhi* (bodily perfection with strength, firmness, beauty and grace). –52.

सुषिरं ज्ञानजनकं पञ्चस्त्रोतः समन्वितम् ।
तिष्ठते खेचरी मुद्रा तस्मिन्शून्ये निरञ्जने ॥५३॥

suṣiraṃ jñānajanakaṃ pañcasrotaḥ samanvitam ।
tiṣṭhate khecarī mudrā tasminśūnye nirañjane ॥53॥

The cavity (*suṣumṇā*) is the giver of knowledge. It is the confluence of five rivers (*nāḍīs – iḍā, piṅgalā, suṣumṇā, gandhāri* and *hastijihva*) coming together here. In the space (void) of that hole free from any taint (of ignorance or delusion), the *khecarī mudrā* should be established. –53.

एकं सृष्टिमयं बीजमेका मुद्रा च खेचरी ।
एको देवो निरालम्ब एकावस्था मनोन्मनी ॥५४॥

ekaṃ sṛṣṭimayaṃ bījamekā mudrā ca khecarī ।
eko devo nirālamba ekāvasthā manonmanī ॥54॥

There is only one *bīja* (literally, the seed) from which the whole universe evolves. There is only one *mudrā* - *khecarī*. There is only one *deva* (god) without any support. There is only one *avasthā* (state), it is *manonmanī* (the state beyond mind). –54.

Practice of Uḍḍiyāna Bandha

अथ उड्डीयानबन्धः ।

बद्धो येन सुषुम्णायां प्राणस्तूड्डीयते यतः ।

तस्मादुड्डीयनाख्योऽयं योगिभिः समुदाहृतः ॥५५॥

atha uḍḍīyānabandhaḥ ।

Now *uḍḍiyāna bandha* is described.

baddho yena suṣumṇāyāṃ prāṇastūḍḍīyate yataḥ ।

tasmāduḍḍīyanākhyo'yaṃ yogibhiḥ samudāhṛtaḥ ॥55॥

By this *bandha*, the *prāṇa* flies through the *suṣumṇā*. This is why it is called *uḍḍiyāna bandha* by the yogīs. –55.

उड्डीनं कुरुते यस्मादविश्रान्तं महाखगः ।

उड्डीयानं तदेव स्यात्तव बन्धोऽभिधीयते ॥५६॥

uḍḍīnaṃ kurute yasmādaviśrāntaṃ mahākhagaḥ ।

uḍḍīyānaṃ tadeva syāttattra bandho'bhidhīyate ॥56॥

This *bandha* is known as *uḍḍiyāna* (i.e. the 'flying *bandha*') because the restless great bird (*śakti*) flies up (through the middle channel – i.e. *suṣumṇā*). –56.

उदरे पश्चिमं तानं नाभेरूर्ध्वं च कारयेत् ।

उड्डीयानो ह्यसौ बन्धो मृत्युमातङ्गकेसरी ॥५७॥

udare paścimaṃ tānaṃ nābherūrdhvaṃ ca kārayet ।

uḍḍīyāno hyaso bandho mṛtyumātaṅgakesarī ॥57॥

Drawing the abdomen, along with the area above the navel, up (towards the spine and ribcage) is called *uḍḍiyāna bandha*. This *bandha* is like a lion that defeats the elephant (i.e. death). –57.

उड्डीयानं तु सहजं गुरुणा कथितं सदा ।

अभ्यसेत्सततं यस्तु वृद्धोऽपि तरुणायते ॥५८॥

uḍḍīyānaṃ tu sahajaṃ guruṇā kathitaṃ sadā ।

abhyasetsatataṃ yastu vṛddho'pi taruṇāyate ॥58॥

The practice of *uḍḍiyāna bandha*, as taught by a guru, always becomes natural. Through its constant practice, even an old man becomes young. –58.

नाभेरुर्ध्वमधश्चापि तानं कुर्यात्प्रयत्नतः ।

षण्मासमभ्यसेन्मृत्युं जयत्येव न संशयः ॥५९॥

nābherūrdhvamadhaścāpi tānaṃ kuryātprayatnataḥ ।

ṣaṇmāsamabhyasenmṛtyuṃ jayatyeva na saṃśayaḥ ॥59॥

The area above and below the navel should be drawn back with effort. By practicing this for six months, death will be conquered. There is no doubt about it. –59.

सर्वेषामेव बन्धानां उत्तमो ह्युड्डीयानकः ।

उड्डियाने दृढे बन्धे मुक्तिः स्वाभाविकी भवेत् ॥६०॥

sarveṣāmeva bandhānāmuttamo hyuḍḍīyānakaḥ ।

uḍḍiyāne dṛḍhe bandhe muktiḥ svābhāvikī bhavet ॥60॥

Of all the *bandhas*, *uḍḍiyāna bandha* is the most excellent. When mastery is gained over this *bandha*, *mukti* (liberation) follows naturally. –60.

Practice of Mūla Bandha

अथ मूलबन्धः ।

पार्ष्णिभागेन सम्पीड्य योनिमाकुञ्चयेद्गुदम् ।

अपानमूर्ध्वमाकृष्य मूलबन्धोऽभिधीयते ॥६१॥

atha mūlabandhaḥ ।

Now *mūla bandha* is described.

pārṣṇibhāgena sampīḍya yonimākuñcayedgudam ।

apānamūrdhvamākṛṣya mūlabandho'bhidhīyate ॥61॥

Pressing the perineum with the heel, contract the anus and draw the *apāna vāyu* upwards. This is called *mūla bandha*. –61.

अधोगतिमपानं वा ऊर्ध्वगं कुरुते बलात् ।

आकुञ्चनेन तं प्राहुर्मूलबन्धं हि योगिनः ॥६२॥

adhogatimapānaṃ vā ūrdhvagaṃ kurute balāt ।

ākuñcanena taṃ prāhurmūlabandhaṃ hi yoginaḥ ॥62॥

The downward moving *apāna vāyu* is forced to move upward by contracting the perineum. This is called *mūla bandha* by the yogīs. –62.

गुदं पार्ष्ण्या तु सम्पीड्य वायुमाकुञ्चयेद्बलात् ।

वारं वारं यथा चोर्ध्वं समायाति समीरणः ॥६३॥

gudaṃ pārṣṇyā tu sampīḍya vāyumākuñcayedbalāt ।

vāraṃvāraṃ yathā cordhvaṃ samāyāti samīraṇaḥ ॥63॥

Pressing the anus firmly with the heel, contract the *vāyu* forcibly and repeatedly so that the *vāyu* (*apāna*) moves upwards. –63.

प्राणापानौ नादबिन्दू मूलबन्धेन चैकताम् ।

गत्वा योगस्य संसिद्धिं यच्छतो नात्र संशयः ॥६४॥

prāṇāpānau nādabindū mūlabandhena caikatām ।

gatvā yogasya saṃsiddhiṃ yacchato nātra saṃśayaḥ ॥64॥

Through the practice of *mūla bandha*, *prāṇa* and *apāna*, *nāda* and *bindu* are united. It gives complete perfection in yoga. There is no doubt about it. –64.

अपानप्राणयोरैक्यं क्षयो मूत्रपुरीषयोः ।

युवा भवति वृद्धोऽपि सततं मूलबन्धनात् ॥६५॥

apānaprāṇayoraikyaṃ kṣayo mūtrapurīṣayoḥ ।

yuvā bhavati vṛddho'pi satataṃ mūlabandhanāt ॥65॥

By constant practice of *mūla bandha*, *prāṇa* and *apāna* are united, and excretions of urine and excrement are reduced. Even an old person becomes youthful. –65.

अपान ऊर्ध्वगे जाते प्रयाते वह्निमण्डलम् ।

तदानलशिखा दीर्घा जायते वायुनाहता ॥६६॥

apāna ūrdhvage jāte prayāte vahnimaṇḍalam ।

tadā'nalaśikhā dīrghā jāyate vāyunā'hatā ॥66॥

When the *apāna* moves upwards and reaches the region of fire (*maṇipura cakra*), then the flame of the fire grows long, being blown by *apāna vāyu*. –66.

ततो यातो वह्न्यपानौ प्राणमुष्णस्वरूपकम् ।

तेनात्यन्तप्रदीप्तस्तु ज्वलनो देहजस्तथा ॥६७॥

tato yāto vahnyapānau prāṇamuṣṇasvarūpakam ।

tenātyantapradīptastu jvalano dehajastathā ॥67॥

When there is a union of *apāna* and fire with prāṇa that is naturally hot, then the heat in the body is highly increased and the fire burns vigorously. –67.

तेन कुण्डलिनी सुप्ता सन्तप्ता सम्प्रबुध्यते ।

दण्डाहता भुजङ्गीव निश्वस्य ऋजुतां व्रजेत् ॥६८॥

tena kuṇḍalinī suptā santaptā samprabudhyate ।

daṇḍāhatā bhujanggīva niśvasya ṛjutāṃ vrajet ॥68॥

Due to that, the sleeping *Kuṇḍalinī* is awakened by the intense heat, just as a serpent beaten with a stick hisses and straightens itself. –68.

बिलं प्रविष्टेव ततो ब्रह्मनाड्यंतरं व्रजेत् ।

तस्मान्नित्यं मूलबन्धः कर्तव्यो योगिभिः सदा ॥६९॥

bilaṃ praviṣṭeva tato brahmanāḍyantaraṃ vrajet ।

tasmānnityaṃ mūlabandhaḥ kartavyo yogibhiḥ sadā ॥69॥

In this way, just as a snake goes in its hole, the *kuṇḍalinī* enters into the *brahma nāḍī* (psychic channel *suṣumṇā* which leads to *Brahma*) therefore, it is the duty of the yogī to always perform *mūla bandha*. –69.

Practice of Jālandhara Bandha

अथ जलन्धर-बन्धः ।

कण्ठमाकुञ्च्य हृदये स्थापयेच्चिबुकं दृढम् ।

बन्धो जालन्धराख्योऽयं जरामृत्युविनाशकः ॥७०॥

atha jālandharabandhaḥ ।

Now *jālandhara bandha* is described.

kaṇṭhamākuñcya hṛdaye sthāpayeccibukaṃ dṛḍham ।

bandho jālandharākhyo'yaṃ jarāmṛtyuvināśakaḥ ॥*70*॥

Contract the throat and press the chin firmly against the chest. This is called *jālandhara bandha* (i.e. the throat lock), the destroyer of old age and death. –70.

बध्नाति हि सिराजालमधोगामि नभोजलम् ।

ततो जालन्धरो बन्धः कण्ठदुःखौघनाशनः ॥७१॥

badhnāti hi sirājālamadhogāmi nabhojalam ।

tato jālandharo bandhaḥ kaṇṭhaduḥkhaughanāśanaḥ ॥*71*॥

Verily, it tightens the network of *nāḍīs* and stops downward flow of nectar (from the moon). So, it is called *jālandhara bandha*, the destroyer of all throat ailments. –71.

जालन्धरे कृते बन्धे कण्ठसंकोचलक्षणे ।

न पीयूषं पतत्यग्नौ न च वायुः प्रकुप्यति ॥७२॥

jālandhare kṛte bandhe kaṇṭhasaṅkocalakṣaṇe ।

na pīyūṣaṃ patatyagnau na ca vāyuḥ prakupyati ॥*72*॥

When the *jālandhara bandha* is performed by contraction of the throat, the nectar does not fall into the (digestive) fire and the *prāṇa* is not excited. –72.

कण्ठसंकोचनेनैव द्वे नाड्यौ स्तम्भयेद्दृढम् ।

मध्यचक्रमिदं ज्ञेयं षोडशाधारबन्धनम् ॥७३॥

kaṇṭhasaṅkocanenaiva dve nāḍyau stambhayeddṛḍham ।

madhyacakramidāṃ jñeyaṃ ṣoḍaśādhārabandhanam ॥*73*॥

The two *nāḍīs* (*idā* and *piṅgalā*) should be stopped firmly by contracting the throat. This is called the middle center or *viśuddhi cakra* that locks or binds the sixteen *adhāras* (vital supports of the body). –73.

मूलस्थानं समाकुञ्च्य उड्डियानं तु कारयेत् ।

इडां च पिङ्गलां बद्ध्वा वाहयेत्पश्चिमे पथि ॥७४॥

mūlasthānaṃ samākuñcya uḍḍiyānaṃ tu kārayet ।

iḍāṃ ca piṅgalāṃ baddhvā vāhayetpaścime pathi ॥74॥

By contracting the perineum (*mūla bandha*), the *uḍḍiyāna bandha* should be performed. By firmly locking the *idā* and *piṅgalā* (with *jālandhara bandha*) the breath (*prāṇa*) should be directed through the posterior path (*suṣumṇā*). –74.

अनेनैव विधानेन प्रयाति पवनो लयम् ।

ततो न जायते मृत्युर्जरारोगादिकं तथा ॥७५॥

anenaivavidhānena prayāti pavano layam ।

tato na jāyate mṛtyurjarārogādikaṃ tathā ॥75॥

By these means the *prāṇa* is dissolved (i.e. becomes calm and still). Thus, death, old age and diseases are eliminated. –75.

बन्धत्रयमिदं श्रेष्ठं महासिद्धैश्च सेवितम् ।

सर्वेषां हठतन्त्राणां साधनं योगिनो विदुः ॥७६॥

bandhatrayamidāṃ śreṣṭhaṃ mahāsiddhaiśca sevitam ।

sarveṣāṃ haṭhatantrāṇāṃ sādhanaṃ yogino viduḥ ॥76॥

These three *bandhas* (the locks) are excellent and are performed by the great *siddhas*. Of all the means of practice in *Haṭha Yoga* and *Tantra*, yogīs know them as the best ones. –76.

यत्किंचित्स्रवते चन्द्रादमृतं दिव्यरूपिणः ।

तत्सर्वं ग्रसते सूर्यस्तेन पिण्डो जरायुतः ॥७७॥

yatkiñcitsravate candrādamṛtaṃ divyarūpiṇaḥ ।

tatsarvaṃ grasate sūryastena piṇḍo jarāyutaḥ ॥77॥

The nectar that flows from the moon has divine quality. It is all normally burned up by the fire of the sun. Therefore, the body becomes old. –77.

Practice of Viparīta Karaṇī Mudrā

अथ विपरीतकरणी ।

मुद्रा तत्रास्ति करणं दिव्यं सूर्यस्य मुखवञ्चनम् ।

गुरूपदेशतो ज्ञेयं न तु शास्त्रार्थकोटिभिः ॥७८॥

atha viparītakaraṇī ।

Now *viparīta karaṇī mudrā* is described.

tatrāsti karaṇaṃ divyaṃ sūryasya mukhavañcanam ।

gurūpadeśato jñeyaṃ na tu śāstrārthakoṭibhiḥ ॥78॥

There is a divine means by which the mouth of the sun is blocked (so that the nectar is prevented from falling into it). This should be learnt from the instructions of the guru and certainly not by (theoretical) study, debate and discussion of millions of *śāstras* (the scriptures). –78.

ऊर्ध्वनाभेरधस्तालोरूर्ध्वं भानुरधः शशी ।

करणी विपरीताखा गुरुवाक्येन लभ्यते ॥७९॥

ūrdhvaṃ nābheradhastālorūrdhvaṃ bhānuradhaḥ śaśī ।

karaṇī viparītākhyā guruvākyena labhyate ॥79॥

This is called *viparīta karaṇī mudrā* (inverted attitude) when the navel region is above and the palate is below, and the sun is above and the moon is below. It should be learnt from the instructions of the guru. –79.

नित्यमभ्यासयुक्तस्य जठराग्निविवर्धिनी ।

आहारो बहुलस्तस्य सम्पाद्यः साधकस्य च ॥८०॥

nityamabhyāsayuktasya jaṭharāgnivivardhinī ।

āhāro bahulastasya sampādyaḥ sādhakasya ca ॥80॥

He who practices it regularly every day, his digestive fire is stimulated. Therefore, the practitioner should perform it while he has a sufficient stock of food. –80.

अल्पाहारो यदि भवेदग्निर्दहति तत्क्षणात् ।

अधःशिराश्चोर्ध्वपादः क्षणं स्यात्प्रथमे दिने ॥८१॥

alpāhāro yadi bhavedagnirdahati tatkṣaṇāt ।

adhaḥ śirāścordhvapādaḥ kṣaṇaṃ syātprathame dine ॥81॥

If he takes only a little food, the (digestive) fire consumes everything right away. Therefore, on the first day (of practice) one should stay only for a moment keeping the head down and the feet up. –81.

क्षणाच्च किंचिदधिकमभ्यसेच्च दिने दिने ।

वलितं पलितं चैव षण्मासोर्ध्वं न दृश्यते ।

याममात्रं तु यो नित्यमभ्यसेत्स तु कालजित् ॥८२॥

kṣaṇāñca kiñcidādhikabhyaseñca dine dine ।

valitaṃ palitaṃ caiva ṣaṇmāsordhvaṃ na dṛśyate ।

yāmamātraṃ tu yo nityamabhyasetsa tu kālajit ॥82॥

It should be performed daily – gradually increasing the duration of practice. Over six months, grey hairs and wrinkles will disappear. He who practices it for a *yama* (three hours) daily, he becomes the conqueror of death. –82.

Practice of Vajrolī Mudrā

अथ वज्रोली ।

स्वेच्छया वर्तमानोऽपि योगोक्तैर्नियमैर्विना ।

वज्रोलीं यो विजानाति स योगी सिद्धिभाजनम् ॥८३॥

atha vajrolī ।

Now *vajrolī* is described.

svecchayā vartamāno'pi yogoktairniyamairvinā ।

vajrolīṃ yo vijānāti sa yogī siddhibhājanam ॥83॥

Even a householder living a free lifestyle without following any prescribed rules of yoga, if he knows *vajrolī* well, he is a yogī and he deserves to achieve all *siddhis*. –83.

तत्र वस्तुद्वयं वक्ष्ये दुर्लभं यस्य कस्यचित् ।

क्षीरं चैकं द्वितीयं तु नारी च वशवर्तिनी ॥८४॥

tatra vastudvayaṃ vakṣye durlabhaṃ yasya kasyacit ।

kṣīraṃ caikaṃ dvitīyaṃ tu nārī ca vaśavartinī ॥84॥

There are two things very difficult to obtain for this (practice). One is milk and another is a woman (partner) who can serve।act according to one's wishes. –84.

मेहनेन शनैः सम्यगूर्ध्वाकुञ्चनमभ्यसेत् ।

पुरुषोऽप्यथवा नारी वज्रोलीसिद्धिमाप्नुयात् ॥८५॥

mehanena śanaiḥ samyagūrdhvākuñcanamabhyaset ।

puruṣo'pyathavā nārī vajrolīsiddhimāpnuyāt ॥85॥

One should gradually perform upward contractions of the urethra to draw up the *bindu* emitted during intercourse. A man or a woman may attain perfection (in the practice) of *vajrolī* (by doing so). –85.

यत्नतः शस्तनालेन फूत्कारं वज्रकन्दरे ।

शनैः शनैः प्रकुर्वीत वायुसंचारकारणात् ॥८६॥

yatnataḥ śastanālena phūtkāraṃ vajrakandare ।

śanaiḥ śanaiḥ prakurvīta vāyusañcārakāraṇāt ॥86॥

With due effort, slowly draw in air through an excellent tube inserted into the urethra of the penis, and then gradually direct *vāyu* (*prāṇa*) into *vajra kandha* (i.e. the bulbous root). –86.

नारीभगे पदद्बिन्दुमभ्यासेनोर्ध्वमाहरेत् ।

चलितं च निजं बिन्दुमूर्ध्वमाकृष्य रक्षयेत् ॥८७॥

nārībhage patadbindumabhyāsenordhvamāharet ।

calitaṃ ca nijaṃ bindumūrdhvamākṛṣya rakṣayet ॥87॥

The seminal fluid that is about to emit into the vagina of the woman should be drawn upward by practice. Should it fall, both the partners (male and female) should preserve their *bindu* (the seminal fluid।ovarian fluid) by drawing it up. –87.

एवं संरक्षयेद्बिन्दुं जयति योगवित् ।

मरणं बिन्दुपातेन जीवनं बिन्दुधारणात् ॥८८॥

evaṃ saṃrakṣayedbinduṃ jayati yogavit ।

maraṇaṃ bindupātena jīvanaṃ bindudhāraṇāt ॥88॥

By preserving the *bindu* in this way, the knower of yoga conquers death. Ejaculation of *bindu* is death. Preservation of *bindu* is life. –88.

सुगन्धो योगिनो देहे जायते बिन्दुधारणात् ।

यावद्बिन्दुः स्थिरो देहे तावत्कालभयं कुतः ॥८९॥

sugandho yogino dehe jāyate bindudhāraṇāt ।

yāvadbinduḥ sthiro dehe tāvat kālabhayaṃ kutaḥ ॥89॥

By the preservation of the *bindu* the body of the yogī smells sweet. So long as the *bindu* is stable in the body, then where is the fear of death? –89.

चित्तायत्तं नृणां शुक्रं शुक्रायत्तं च जीवितम् ।

तस्माच्छुक्रं मनश्चैव रक्षणीयं प्रयत्नतः ॥९०॥

cittāyattaṃ nṛṇāṃ śukraṃ śukrāyattaṃ ca jīvitam ।

tasmācchukraṃ manaścaiva rakṣaṇīyaṃ prayatnataḥ ॥90॥

A man's seminal fluid is under control of the mind and control of seminal fluid is life-giving (i.e. life-force is dependent on the seminal fluid). Therefore, the seminal fluid and the mind should be preserved and controlled with due effort. –90.

ऋतुमत्या रजोऽप्येवं निजं बिन्दुं च रक्षयेत् ।

मेढ्रेणाकर्षयेदूर्ध्वं सम्यगभ्यासयोगवित् ॥९१॥

ṛtumatyā rajo'pyevaṃ nijaṃ binduṃ ca rakṣayet ।

meḍhreṇākarṣayedūrdhvaṃ samyagabhyāsayogavit ॥91॥

The knower of yoga who is perfect in practice should preserve his *bindu* as well as the *rāja* (ovarian fluid of a woman gone through her menstrual cycle) by drawing it upward through his genital organ. –91.

Practice of Sahajolī Mudrā

अथ सहजोलिः ।

सहजोलिश्चामरोलिर्वज्रोल्या भेद एकतः ।

जले सुभस्म निक्षिप्य दग्धगोमयसम्भवम् ॥९२॥

atha sahajoliḥ ।

Now *Sahajolī mudrā* is described.

sahajoliścāmarolirvajrolyā bheda ekataḥ ।

jale subhasma nikṣipya dagdhagomayasambhavam ॥92॥

Sahajolī and *amarolī* are the modifications or variations (of the practice) of *vajrolī*. The burnt ashes of cow-dung should be mixed with water. -92.

वज्रोलीमैथुनादूर्ध्वं स्त्रीपुंसोः स्वाङ्गलेपनम् ।

आसीनयोः सुखेनैव मुक्तव्यापारयोः क्षणात् ॥९३॥

vajrolīmaithunādūrdhvaṃ strīpuṃsoḥ svāṅgalepanam ।

āsīnayoḥ sukhenaiva muktavyāpārayoḥ kṣaṇāt ॥93॥

After performing *vajrolī* intercourse, both the man and woman should smear the ashes on (parts of) their bodies. Being finished with the practice of *vajrolī*, this should be done in a comfortable position. –93.

सहजोलिरियं प्रोक्ता श्रद्धेया योगिभिः सदा ।

अयं शुभकरो योगो भोगयुक्तोऽपि मुक्तिदः ॥९४॥

sahajoliriyaṃ proktā śraddheyā yogibhiḥ sadā ।

ayaṃ śubhakaro yogo bhogayukto'pi muktidāḥ ॥94॥

This is called *sahajolī*, and the yogīs always have faith in it. This is auspicious yoga and gives one *mukti* (liberation) even if he is engaged in *bhoga* (sensual enjoyment). –94.

अयं योगः पुण्यवतां धीराणां तत्त्वदर्शिनाम् ।

निर्मत्सराणां वै सिध्येन्न तु मत्सरशालिनाम् ॥९५॥

ayaṃ yogaḥ puṇyavatāṃ dhīrāṇāṃ tattvadarśinām ।

nirmatsarāṇāṃ vai sidhyenna tu matsaraśālinām ॥95॥

This yoga is attained by those men who are virtuous, courageous and selfless, and who have realized the truth, and certainly not by those who are engaged in selfish activities. –95.

Practice of Amarolī

अथ अमरोली ।

पित्तोल्बणत्वात्प्रथमाम्बुधारां विहाय निःसारतयान्त्यधाराम् ।

निषेव्यते शीतलमध्यधारा कापालिके खण्डमतेऽमरोली ॥९६॥

atha amarolī ।

Now *amarolī* is described.

pittolbaṇatvātprathamāmbudhārāṃ

vihāya niḥsāratayāntyadhārām ।

niṣevyate śītalamadhyadhārā

kāpālike khaṇḍamate'marolī ॥96॥

According to the belief of the *kapālika* sect, *amarolī* involves the practice of drinking cool midstream urine. The first part of the urine is left as it contains excessive bile and the last part is left, as it has no essence. –96.

अमरीं यः पिबेन्नित्यं नस्यं कुर्वन्दिने दिने ।

वज्रोलीमभ्यसेत्सम्यक्सामरोलीति कथ्यते ॥९७॥

amarīṃ yaḥ pibennityaṃ nasyaṃ kurvandine dine ।

vajrolīmabhyasetsamyaksāmarolīti kathyate ॥97॥

He who regularly drinks *amarī*, takes snuff of the urine daily, and performs *vajrolī*; he is said to be rightly practicing *amarolī*. –97.

अभ्यासान्निःसृतां चान्द्रीं विभूत्या सह मिश्रयेत् ।

धारयेदुत्तमाङ्गेषु दिव्यदृष्टिः प्रजायते ॥९८॥

abhyāsānniḥsṛtāṃ cāndrīṃ vibhūtyā saha miśrayet ।

dhārayeduttamāṅgeṣu divyadṛṣṭiḥ prajāyate ॥98॥

The *bindu* discharged during the practice of *vajrolī* should be mixed with sacred ashes and rubbed on the best parts of the body. It confers divine vision. –98.

पुंसो बिन्दुं समाकुञ्च्य सम्यगभ्यासपाटवात् ।
यदि नारी रजो रक्षेद्वज्रोल्या सापि योगिनी ॥९९॥

puṃso binduṃ samākuñcya samyagabhyāsapāṭavāt ।
yadi nārī rajo rakṣedvajrolyā sāpi yogini ॥99॥

If a woman preserves her *raja* (the ovarian fluid) by the practice of *vajrolī* and the *bindu* (the seminal fluid of a man) through the proficient practice of right contraction, she is also a *yoginī*. –99.

तस्याः किंचिद्रजो नाशं न गच्छति न संशयः ।
तस्याः शरीरे नादश्च बिन्दुतामेव गच्छति ॥१००॥

tasyāḥ kiñcidrajo nāśaṃ na gacchati na saṃśayaḥ ।
tasyāḥ śarīre nādaśca bindutāmeva gacchati ॥100॥

Her *raja* is not lost at all. There is no doubt about it. The *nāda* takes the form of the *bindu* in her body (i.e. it becomes one with *bindu* ।identical to *bindu*). –100.

स बिन्दुस्तद्रजश्चैव एकीभूय स्वदेहगौ ।
वज्रोल्यभ्यासयोगेन सर्वसिद्धिं प्रयच्छतः ॥१०१॥

sa bindustadrājaścaiva ekībhūya svadehagau ।
vajrolyabhyāsayogena sarvasiddhiṃ prayacchataḥ ॥101॥

By the practice of *vajrolī* both the *bindu* and *raja* are united in the body. This bestows all *siddhis* (perfections). –101.

रक्षेदाकुञ्चनादूर्ध्वं या रजः सा हि योगिनी ।
अतीतानागतं वेत्ति खेचरी च भवेद्ध्रुवम् ॥१०२॥

rakṣedākuñcanādūrdhvaṃ yā rājaḥ sā hi yoginī ।
atītānāgataṃ vetti khecarī ca bhaveddhruvam ॥102॥

She who protects her *raja* drawing it upwards through the contraction (of her *yoni*) is truly a *yoginī*. She knows the past, present and future and certainly, attains perfection in *khecarī mudrā*. –102.

देहसिद्धिं च लभते वज्रोल्यभ्यासयोगतः ।

अयं पुण्यकरो योगो भोगे भुक्तेऽपि मुक्तिदः ॥१०३॥

dehasiddhiṃ ca labhate vajrolyabhyāsayogataḥ ।

ayaṃ puṇyakaro yogo bhoge bhukte'pi muktidāḥ ॥103॥

The practitioner attains *deha siddhi* (perfection of the body) through the constant practice of *vajrolī* yoga. This auspicious yoga even confers liberation despite sensual enjoyments of worldly objects. –103.

Śakti Cālana Mudrā

अथ शक्तिचालनम् ।

कुटिलाङ्गी कुण्डलिनी भुजङ्गी शक्तिरीश्वरी ।

कुण्डल्यरुन्धती चैते शब्दाः पर्यायवाचकाः ॥१०४॥

atha śakticālanam ।

Now *śakti cālana* is described.

kuṭilāṅgī kuṇḍalinī bhujaṅgī śaktirīśvarī ।

kuṇḍalyarundhatī caite śabdāḥ paryāyavācakāḥ ॥104॥

Kuṭilāṅgī, Kuṇḍalinī, Bhujaṅgī, Śakti, Īśvarī, Kuṇḍalī and *Arundhatī* are all synonymous names of the same *Kuṇḍalinī Śakti*. –104.

उद्घाटयेत्कपाटं तु यथा कुंचिकया हठात् ।

कुण्डलिन्या तथा योगी मोक्षद्वारं विभेदयेत् ॥१०५॥

udghāṭayetkapāṭaṃ tu yathā kuñcikayā haṭhāt ।

kuṇḍalinyā tathā yogī mokṣadvāraṃ vibhedayet ॥105॥

Just as a door is suddenly opened with a key, so should the yogī open the doorway to liberation with *Kuṇḍalinī Śakti*. –105.

येन मार्गेण गन्तव्यं ब्रह्मस्थानं निरामयम् ।

मुखेनाच्छाद्य तद्वारं प्रसुप्ता परमेश्वरी ॥१०६॥

yena mārgeṇa gantavyaṃ brahmasthānaṃ nirāmayam ।

mukhenācchādya tadvāraṃ prasuptā parameśvarī ॥106॥

The *Parameśvarī* is asleep, closing the mouth of the path by which one should go to *Brahmasthāna* (the abode of *Brahma*) – that is free from disease, death, or pain. –106.

कन्दोर्ध्वं कुण्डली शक्तिः सुप्ता मोक्षाय योगिनाम् ।

बन्धनाय च मूढानां यस्तां वेत्ति स योगवित् ॥१०७॥

kandordhvaṃ kuṇḍalī śaktiḥ suptā mokṣāya yogināṃ ।

bandhanāya ca mūḍhānāṃ yastāṃ vetti sa yogavit ॥107॥

The *Kuṇḍalinī* sleeps above the *kanda* (the bulbous root). This *Śakti* gives liberation to the yogīs and bondage to the ignorant. He who knows her is the knower of yoga. - 107.

कुण्डली कुटिलाकारा सर्पवत्परिकीर्तिता ।

सा शक्तिश्चालिता येन स मुक्तो नात्र संशयः ॥१०८॥

kuṇḍalī kuṭilākārā sarpavatparikīrtitā ।

sā śaktiścālitā yena sa mukto nātra saṃśayaḥ ॥108॥

It is described that *Kuṇḍalinī* has a curved shape, and is coiled like a snake. He, who makes that *Śakti* move upwards, attains liberation without doubt. – 108.

गङ्गायमुनयोर्मध्ये बालरण्डां तपस्विनीम् ।

बलात्कारेण गृह्णीयात्तद्विष्णोः परमं पदम् ॥१०९॥

gaṅgāyamunayormadhye bālaraṇḍāṃ tapasvinīm ।

balātkāreṇa gṛhṇīyāttadviṣṇoḥ paramaṃ padam ॥109॥

Between the *Gaṅgā* and the *Yamunā*, there resides *Bālaraṇḍā* (literally, a young widow) performing austerity. She should be seized by force in order to get the highest state of *Viṣṇu*. –109.

इडा भगवती गङ्गा पिङ्गला यमुना नदी ।

इडापिङ्गलयोर्मध्ये बालरण्डा च कुण्डली ॥११०॥

iḍā bhagavatī gaṅgā piṅgalā yamunā nadī ।

iḍāpiṅgalayormadhye bālaraṇḍā ca kuṇḍalī ॥110॥

Idā is the holy *Gaṅgā* and *piṅgalā* is the holy river *Yamunā*. In the middle of *idā* and *piṅgalā* (i.e. the lunar and solar psychic pathways respectively) dwells the young widow, the *Kuṇḍalinī*. –110.

पुच्छे प्रगृह्य भुजङ्गीं सुप्तामुद्बोधयेच्च ताम् ।

निद्रां विहाय सा शक्तिरूर्ध्वमुत्तिष्ठते हठात् ॥१११॥

pucche pragṛhya bhujaṅgīṃ suptāmudbodhayecca tām ।

nidrāṃ vihāya sā śaktirūrdhvamuttiṣṭhate haṭhāt ॥111॥

By catching her tail, this sleeping serpent should be awakened. The *Śakti* gives up her sleep and suddenly rises upwards. –111.

अवस्थिता चैव फणावती सा प्रातश्च सायं प्रहरार्धमात्रम् ।

प्रपूर्य सूर्यात्परिधानयुक्त्या प्रगृह्य नित्यं परिचालनीया ॥११२॥

avasthitā caiva phaṇāvatī sā

prātaśca sāyaṃ praharārdhamātram ।

prapūrya sūryāt paridhānayuktyā

praghṛhya nityaṃ paricālanīyā ॥112॥

Inhaling through the right nostril (*piṅgalā*), the lying Serpent (*Śakti*) should be grasped and activated everyday in the morning and evening for an hour and a half, following the method of *paridhāna* (a process of rotating the *Śakti* for its awakening). –112.

ऊर्ध्वं वितस्तिमात्रं तु विस्तारं चतुरङ्गुलम् ।

मृदुलं धवलं प्रोक्तं वेष्टिताम्बरलक्षणम् ॥११३॥

ūrdhvaṃ vitastimātraṃ tu vistāraṃ caturaṅgulam ।

mṛdulaṃ dhavalaṃ proktaṃ veṣṭitāmbaralakṣaṇam ॥113॥

The *kanda* (bulbous root where all the *nāḍīs* are joined together) above the anus is one hand span (twelve inches) high and four fingers wide. It is described that it is soft and white, and looks as if wrapped in folded cloth. –113.

सति वज्रासने पादौ कराभ्यां धारयेद्दृढम् ।

गुल्फदेशसमीपे च कन्दं तत्र प्रपीडयेत् ॥११४॥

sati vajrāsane pādau karābhyāṃ dhārayeddṛḍham ।

gulphadeśasamīpe ca kandaṃ tatra prapīḍayet ॥114॥

Sitting in the *vajrāsana* (*siddhāsana*) posture, firmly take hold of the ankles. Press very hard on the area close to the ankles where the *kanda* is located. –114.

Quick Awakening of the Kuṇḍalinī

वज्रासने स्थितो योगी चालयित्वा च कुण्डलीम् ।

कुर्यादनन्तरं भस्त्रां कुण्डलीमाशु बोधयेत् ॥११५॥

vajrāsane sthito yogī cālayitvā ca kuṇḍalīm ।

kuryādanantaraṃ bhastrāṃ kuṇḍalīmāśu bodhayet ॥115॥

Remaining in the position of *vajrāsana*, the yogī should move the *Kuṇḍalinī*. During this practice he should perform *bhastrikā prāṇāyāma*. This awakens the *Kuṇḍalinī* quickly. –115.

भानोराकुञ्चनं कुर्यात्कुण्डलीं चालयेत्ततः ।

मृत्युवक्त्रगतस्यापि तस्य मृत्युभयं कुतः ॥११६॥

bhānorākuñcanaṃ kuryātkuṇḍalīṃ cālayettataḥ ।

mṛtyuvaktragatasyāpi tasya mṛtyubhayaṃ kutaḥ ॥116॥

He should contract the sun in *manipura cakra*, then move the *Kuṇḍalinī*. Even though he has entered into the mouth of death, where is the fear of death in him? –116.

मुहूर्तद्वयपर्यन्तं निर्भयं चालनादसौ ।

ऊर्ध्वमाकृष्यते किंचित्सुषुम्णायां समुद्गता ॥११७॥

muhūrtadvayaparyantaṃ nirbhayaṃ cālanādasau ।

ūrdhvamākṛṣyate kiñcitsuṣumṇāyāṃ samudgatā ॥117॥

By moving the *Kuṇḍalinī* fearlessly for an hour and a half, she is drawn upwards and enters a little into the *suṣumṇā*. –117.

तेन कुण्डलिनी तस्याः सुषुम्णाया मुखं ध्रुवम् ।

जहाति तस्मात्प्राणोऽयं सुषुम्णां व्रजति स्वतः ॥११८॥

tena kuṇḍalinī tasyāḥ suṣumṇāyā mukhaṃ dhruvam ।

jahāti tasmātprāṇo'yaṃ suṣumṇāṃ vrājati svataḥ ॥118॥

In this way, the *Kuṇḍalinī* indeed leaves the mouth of the *suṣumṇā* open. Thus the *prāṇa* is able to move through *suṣumṇā* naturally. –118.

तस्मात्संचालयेन्नित्यं सुखसुप्तामरुन्धतीम् ।

तस्याः संचालनेनैव योगी रोगैः प्रमुच्यते ॥११९॥

tasmātsañcālayennityaṃ sukhasuptāmarundhatīm ।

tasyāḥ sañcālanenaiva yogī rogaiḥ pramucyate ॥*119*॥

Therefore, the quietly sleeping *Arundhati* (*Kuṇḍalinī*) should be moved daily. By her regular movement the yogī becomes free from all diseases. –119.

येन संचालिता शक्तिः स योगी सिद्धिभाजनम् ।

किमत्र बहुनोक्तेन कालं जयति लीलया ॥१२०॥

yena sañcālitā śaktiḥ sa yogī siddhibhājanam ।

kimatra bahunoktena kālaṃ jayati līlayā ॥*120*॥

The yogī who moves the *Śakti* becomes the receiver of perfections. What more is there to describe? He easily conquers time (death). –120.

Perfection in Forty Days

ब्रह्मचर्यरतस्यैव नित्यं हितमिताशिनः ।

मण्डलाद्दृश्यते सिद्धिः कुण्डल्यभ्यासयोगिनः ॥१२१॥

brahmacaryaratasyaiva nityaṃ hitamitāśinaḥ ।
maṇḍalāddṛśyate siddhiḥ kuṇḍalyabhyāsayoginaḥ ॥*121*॥

The yogī, who leads a celibate life and always eats moderate and healthy food, sees his perfections in forty days through the practice of awakening *Kuṇḍalinī*. –121.

कुण्डलीं चालयित्वा तु भस्त्रां कुर्याद्विशेषतः ।

एवमभ्यस्यतो नित्यं यमिनो यमभीः कुतः ॥१२२॥

kuṇḍalīṃ cālayitvā tu bhastrāṃ kuryādviśeṣataḥ ।

evamabhyasyato nityaṃ yamino yamabhīḥ kutaḥ ॥*122*॥

After activating the *Kuṇḍalinī*, he should indeed practice *bhastrikā prāṇāyāma* in particular. The *yami* (self-restrained yogī) who is constantly devoted to practice in this way, there is no fear of death for him? –122.

द्वासप्ततिसहस्राणां नाडीनां मलशोधने ।

कुतः प्रक्षालनोपायः कुण्डल्यभ्यसनादृते ॥१२३॥

dvāsaptatisahasrāṇāṃ nāḍīnāṃ malaśodhane ।

kutaḥ prakṣālanopāyaḥ kuṇḍalyabhyasanādṛte ॥123॥

Besides the practice of arousing the *Kuṇḍalinī*, what other methods are there for cleaning up the impurities of seventy-two thousand *nāḍīs*? –123.

इयं तु मध्यमा नाडी दृढाभ्यासेन योगिनाम् ।

आसनप्राणसंयाममुद्राभिः सरला भवेत् ॥१२४॥

iyaṃ tu madhyamā nāḍī dṛḍhābhyāsena yogināṃ ।

āsanaprāṇasaṃyāmamudrābhiḥ saralā bhavet ॥124॥

This middle *nāḍī* (i.e. the *suṣumṇā*) becomes easy (for the *prāṇa* to enter) by the yogī's steady practice of āsana, *prāṇāyāma*, *mudrā* and concentration. –124.

Importance of Śāmbhavī Mudrā

अभ्यासे तु विनिद्राणां मनो धृत्वा समाधिना ।

रुद्राणी वा परा मुद्रा भद्रां सिद्धिं प्रयच्छति ॥१२५॥

abhyāse tu vinidrāṇāṃ mano dhṛtvā samādhinā ।

rudrāṇī vā parā mudrā bhadrāṃ siddhiṃ prayacchati ॥125॥

Those who are awakened by the practice without sloth and whose minds are absorbed in *samādhi*, receive auspicious perfections through the practice of the excellent *rudrāṇī* (*shāmbhavī*) *mudrā*. –125.

राजयोगं विना पृथ्वी राजयोगं विना निशा ।

राजयोगं विना मुद्रा विचित्रापि न शोभते ॥१२६॥

rājayogaṃ vinā pṛthvī rājayogaṃ vinā niśā ।

rājayogaṃ vinā mudrā vicitrāpi na śobhate ॥126॥

Rāja Yoga without *pṛthvī* (literally, earth, here it means stability in posture), *Rāja Yoga* without *niśā* (literally, night, here it means *kumbhaka*), and also the various *mudrās* without *Rāja Yoga* do not give any beauty (i.e. become useless). –126.

मारुतस्य विधिं सर्वं मनोयुक्तं समभ्यसेत् ।

इतरत्र न कर्तव्या मनोवृत्तिर्मनीषिणा ॥१२७॥

mārutasya vidhiṃ sarvaṃ manoyuktaṃ samabhyaset ।

itaratra na kartavyā manovṛttirmanīṣiṇā ॥127॥

The wise practitioner should go through all methods of *prāṇāyāma* well with the concentrated mind on the practice. The wise practitioner should not let his mind wander in *vṛttis* (mental modifications). –127.

इति मुद्रा दश प्रोक्ता आदिनाथेन शम्भुना ।

एकैका तासु यमिनां महासिद्धिप्रदायिनी ॥१२८॥

iti mudrā daśa proktā ādināthena śambhunā ।

ekaikā tāsu yamināṃ mahāsiddhipradāyinī ॥128॥

Thus *Ādinātha Śambhu* (Primeval Lord *Śiva*) has described these ten *mudrās*. Any one of these *mudrās* grants *mahā siddhis* (great perfections) to the *yami* (self-restrained yogī). –128.

Role of a True Guru or a Svāmī

उपदेशं हि मुद्राणां यो दत्ते साम्प्रदायिकम् ।

स एव श्रीगुरुः स्वामी साक्षादीश्वर एव सः ॥१२९॥

upadeśaṃ hi mudrāṇāṃ yo datte sāmpradāyikam ।

sa eva śrīguruḥ svāmī sākṣādīśvara eva saḥ ॥129॥

He who imparts the knowledge of these *mudrās* handed down by successive guru।disciple tradition is indeed a true guru, a *svāmī* and also an *Īśvara* in the form of human being. –129.

तस्य वाक्यपरो भूत्वा मुद्राभ्यासे समाहितः ।

अणिमादिगुणैः सार्धं लभते कालवञ्चनम् ॥१३०॥

tasya vākyaparo bhūtvā mudrābhyāse samāhitaḥ ।

aṇimādiguṇaiḥ sārdhaṃ labhate kālavañcanam ॥130॥

Being fully devoted to his (guru's) words, and involved in the practice of the *mudrās* with a concentrated mind, one attains the qualities or perfections of *aṇimā*, etc., and also deceives *kāla* (i.e. death।time). –130.

इति हठयोगप्रदीपिकायां तृतीयोपदेशः ।

iti haṭhapradīpikāyāṃ tṛtīyopadeśaḥ ॥

Thus ends the Chapter Three of *Haṭha Yoga Pradīpikā.*

CHAPTER FOUR

चतुर्थोपदेशः

Discourse on Samādhi

Śiva as Nāda, Bindu and Kala

नमः शिवाय गुरवे नादबिन्दुकलात्मने ।

निरञ्जनपदं याति नित्यं तत्र परायणः ॥१॥

namaḥ śivāya gurave nādabindukalātmane ।

nirañjanapadaṃ yāti nityaṃ tatra parāyaṇaḥ ॥1॥

Salutations to *Śiva*, the *Guru* who is in the form of *Nāda* (eternal sound or wave energy), *Bindu* (literally, a dot; point of potential energy or nucleus or creation point) and *Kalā* (transcendental wave of time). One who is dedicated to Him reaches the eternal state of *Nirañjana* (a blissful state free from any fault or taint). –1.

अथेदानीं प्रवक्ष्यामि समाधिक्रममुत्तमम् ।

मृत्युघ्नं च सुखोपायं ब्रह्मानन्दकरं परम् ॥२॥

athedānīṃ pravakṣyāmi samādhikramamuttamam ।

mṛtyughnaṃ ca sukhopāyaṃ brahmānandakaraṃ param ॥2॥

Now I am going to describe the excellent method of *samādhi* which destroys death, is the means of getting happiness, and gives the supreme *brahmānanda* (the bliss of the eternal *Brahman* i.e. the Ultimate Truth). –2.

Various Names of the Highest State

राजयोगः समाधिश्च उन्मनी च मनोन्मनी ।

अमरत्वं लयस्तत्त्वं शून्याशून्यं परं पदम् ॥३॥

अमनस्कं तथाद्वैतं निरालम्बं निरञ्जनम् ।

जीवन्मुक्तिश्च सहजा तुर्या चेत्येकवाचकाः ॥४॥

rājayogaḥ samādhiśca unmanī ca manonmanī ।

amaratvaṃ layastattvaṃ śūnyāśūnyaṃ paraṃ padam ॥3॥

amanaskaṃ tathādvaitaṃ nirālambaṃ nirañjanam ।

jīvanmuktiśca sahajā turyā cetyekavācakāḥ ॥4॥

Rājayoga, *samādhi*, *unmanī*, *manonmanī*, *amaratva*, *laya*, *tattva*, *śūnya*, *aśūnya*, *parampada*, *amanaska*, *advaita*, *nirālamba*, *nirañjana*, *jīvanamukti*, *sahaja* and *turiya* are all synonymous terms meaning one and the same thing. –3-4.

सलिले सैन्धवं यद्वत्साम्यं भजति योगतः ।

तथात्ममनसोरैक्यं समाधिरभिधीयते ॥५॥

salile saindhavaṃ yadvatsāmyaṃ bhajati yogataḥ ।

tathātmamanasoraikyaṃ samādhirabhidhīyate ॥5॥

As salt being dissolved in water becomes one with it, similarly the union of *Ātmā* (the Self) and mind is called *samādhi*. –5.

Prāṇa and Mind Cease in Samādhi

यदा संक्षीयते प्राणो मानसं च प्रलीयते ।

तदा समरसत्वं च समाधिरभिधीयते ॥६॥

yadā saṅkṣīyate prāṇo mānasaṃ ca pralīyate ।

tadā samarasatvaṃ ca samādhirabhidhīyate ॥6॥

When the *prāṇa* is stopped altogether and the mind is dissolved (i.e. in the Self), then there arises a state of harmonious equilibrium which is called *samādhi*. –6.

तत्समं च द्वयोरैक्यं जीवात्मपरमात्मनोः ।

प्रनष्टसर्वसङ्कल्पः समाधिः सोऽभिधीयते ॥७॥

tatsamaṃ ca dvayoraikyaṃ jīvātmaparamātmanoḥ ।

prāṇaṣṭasarvasaṅkalpaḥ samādhiḥ so'bhidhīyate ॥7॥

That state of equilibrium, the union of the *Jīvātma* (the Individual Self) and *Paramātma* (the Universal Self), when all *sankalpas* (the ideas, desires and thoughts) are totally annihilated, is called *samādhi*. –7.

Jñāna, Mukti and Siddhi through Guru

राजयोगस्य माहात्म्यं को वा जानाति तत्त्वतः ।

ज्ञानं मुक्तिः स्थितिः सिद्धिर्गुरुवाक्येन लभ्यते ॥८॥

rājayogasya māhātmyaṃ ko vā jānāti tattvataḥ ।

jñānaṃ muktiḥ sthitiḥ siddhirghuruvākyena labhyate ॥8॥

Who knows the real greatness of *Rāja Yoga*? Knowledge of the truth, liberation, the state of bliss and *siddhis* (the perfections) all are attained through the words of the guru. –8.

दुर्लभो विषयत्यागो दुर्लभं तत्त्वदर्शनम् ।

दुर्लभा सहजावस्था सद्गुरोः करुणां विना ॥९॥

durlabho viṣayatyāgo durlabhaṃ tattvadarśanam ।

durlabhā sahajāvasthā sadguroḥ karuṇāṃ vinā ॥9॥

Without the compassion of the true guru, it is difficult to renounce worldly sense-objects, it is (more) difficult to realize the knowledge of the truth, and it is (most) difficult to attain *sahajāvasthā* (the natural state of *Sat*, *Cit* and *Ānanda* i.e. the Ultimate Truth, Intellect and Bliss). –9.

विविधैरासनैः कुभैर्विचित्रैः करणैरपि ।

प्रबुद्धायां महाशक्तौ प्राणः शून्ये प्रलीयते ॥१०॥

vividhairāsanaiḥ kumbhairvicitraiḥ karaṇairapi ।

prabuddhāyāṃ mahāśaktau prāṇaḥ śūnye pralīyate ॥10॥

When *Mahā Śakti* (the great power) is awakened by means of various postures, different *kumbhakas* and *mudrās*, the *prāṇa* dissolves into *śūnya* (literally, the void - *samādhi*). –10.

उत्पन्नशक्तिबोधस्य त्यक्तनिःशेषकर्मणः ।

योगिनः सहजावस्था स्वयमेव प्रजायते ॥११॥

utpannaśaktibodhasya tyaktaniḥśeṣakarmaṇaḥ ।

yoginaḥ sahajāvasthā svayameva prajāyate ॥11॥

The yogī who has realized the awakening of the *Śakti*, and who has renounced all his remaining karmas, attains *sahajāvasthā* (a natural state of *samādhi*) spontaneously (without any effort). –11.

Eradication of Karmic Effects

सुषुम्णावाहिनि प्राणे शून्ये विशति मानसे ।

तदा सर्वाणि कर्माणि निर्मूलयति योगवित् ॥१२॥

suṣumṇāvāhini prāṇe śūnye viśati mānase ।

tadā sarvāṇi karmāṇi nirmūlayati yogavit ॥12॥

When the *prāṇa* flows in the *suṣumṇā* and the mind enters into *śūnya* (the void), then the wise yogī eradicates (the effects of) all his karmas. –12.

अमराय नमस्तुभ्यं सोऽपि कालस्त्वया जितः ।

पतितं वदने यस्य जगदेतच्चराचरम् ॥१३॥

amarāya namastubhyaṃ so'pi kālastvayā jitaḥ ।

patitaṃ vadane yasya jagadetaccarācaram ॥13॥

Salutation to you all immortal ones, by whom victory has been gained over *kāla* (i.e. death।time) – into whose mouth the whole universe (both movable and unmovable। animate and inanimate) falls. –13.

चित्ते समत्वमापन्ने वायौ व्रजति मध्यमे ।

तदामरोली वज्रोली सहजोली प्रजायते ॥१४॥

citte samatvamāpanne vāyau vrājati madhyame ।

tadā'marolī vajrolī sahajolī prajāyate ॥14॥

When the mind reaches an equanimous state and the *prāṇa* enters *suṣumṇā*, then *amarolī*, *vajrolī* and *sahajolī* are accomplished. –14.

Active Prāṇa Stops Inner Knowledge

ज्ञानं कुतो मनसि सम्भवतीह तावत्

प्राणोऽपि जीवति मनो म्रियते न यावत् ।

प्राणो मनो द्वयमिदं विलयं नयेद्यो

मोक्षं स गच्छति नरो न कथंचिदन्यः ॥१५॥

jñānaṃ kuto manasi sambhavatīha tāvat

prāṇo'pi jīvati mano mriyate na yāvat ।

prāṇo mano dvayamidāṃ vilayaṃ nayedyo

mokṣaṃ sa gacchati naro na kathañcidānyaḥ ॥15॥

How can it be possible to let arise *jñāna* (spiritual knowledge) in the mind, as long as the *prāṇa* is active (living) and the mind is not dead? One who makes both, his *prāṇa* and mind latent, attains liberation. It is not possible (to do so) by any other. –15.

ज्ञात्वा सुषुम्णासद्भेदं कृत्वा वायुं च मध्यगम् ।

स्थित्वा सदैव सुस्थाने ब्रह्मरन्ध्रे निरोधयेत् ॥१६॥

jñātvā suṣumṇāsadbhedaṃ kṛtvā vāyuṃ ca madhyagam ।

sthitvā sadaiva susthāne brahmarandhre nirodhayet ॥16॥

Knowing properly how to penetrate *suṣumṇā* and make the *prāṇa* move through this middle path, the yogī, then always staying in a good place, should restrain his *prāṇa* in *brahmarandhra*. –16.

Suṣumṇā Devours Time।Death

सूर्यचन्द्रमसौ धत्तः कालं रात्रिन्दिवात्मकम् ।

भोक्त्री सुषुम्ना कालस्य गुह्यमेतदुदाहृतम् ॥१७॥

sūryacandramasau dhattaḥ kālaṃ rātrindivātmakam ।

bhoktrī suṣumnā kālasya guhyametadudāhṛtam ॥17॥

The sun and the moon divide (and regulate) time in the form of day and night. *Suṣumṇā* is the devourer of time (death). This is a said secret. –17.

द्वासप्ततिसहस्राणि नाडीद्वाराणि पञ्जरे ।

सुषुम्णा शाम्भवी शक्तिः शेषास्त्वेव निरर्थकाः ॥१८॥

dvāsaptatisahasrāṇi nāḍīdvārāṇi pañjare |

suṣumṇā śāmbhavī śaktiḥ śeṣāstveva nirarthakāḥ ||18||

There are seventy-two thousand *nāḍīs* in this cage (of the body). *Suṣumṇā* is *Śāmbhavī Śakti* and the remaining others i.e. *idā, piṅgalā*, etc. are not so important. –18.

वायुः परिचितो यस्मादग्निना सह कुण्डलीम् ।

बोधयित्वा सुषुम्णायां प्रविशेदनिरोधतः ॥१९॥

vāyuḥ paricito yasmādagninā saha kuṇḍalīm |

bodhayitvā suṣumṇāyāṃ praviśedanirodhataḥ ||19||

When there is mastery over the *vāyu*, then together with the digestive fire, the *Kuṇḍalinī* should be awakened and the *prāṇa* should be made to enter the *suṣumṇā* without any restriction. –19.

सुषुम्णावाहिनि प्राणे सिद्ध्यत्येव मनोन्मनी ।

अन्यथा त्वितराभ्यासाः प्रयासायैव योगिनाम् ॥२०॥

suṣumṇāvāhini prāṇe siddhyatyeva manonmanī |

anyathā tvitarābhyāsāḥ prayāsāyaiva yoginām ||20||

When the *prāṇa* flows through *suṣumṇā*, the state of *manonmanī* is accomplished itself. Efforts to be made for other means of practices become futile for the yogī. –20.

पवनो बध्यते येन मनस्तेनैव बध्यते ।

मनश्च बध्यते येन पवनस्तेन बध्यते ॥२१॥

pavano badhyate yena manastenaiva badhyate |

manaśca badhyate yena pavanastena badhyate ||21||

He, who restrains the breath, also suspends the activities of his mind. He, who has controlled his mind, has also controlled his breath. –21.

Vāsana and Prāṇa Activate the Mind

हेतुद्वयं तु चित्तस्य वासना च समीरणः ।

तयोर्विनष्ट एकस्मिन्तौ द्वावपि विनश्यतः ॥२२॥

hetudvayaṃ tu cittasya vāsanā ca samīraṇaḥ ।

tayorvinaṣṭa ekasmintau dvāvapi vinaśyataḥ ॥22॥

There are two causes (of fluctuation) of *citta* (the mind): one is *vāsana* (desires) and the other is the *prāṇa*. When one of these two is destroyed, the other is also destroyed. –22.

मनो यत्र विलीयेत पवनस्तत्र लीयते ।

पवनो लीयते यत्र मनस्तत्र विलीयते ॥२३॥

mano yatra vilīyeta pavanastatra līyate ।

pavano līyate yatra manastatra vilīyate ॥23॥

Where the mind is dissolved, there the *prāṇa* is suspended; and where the *prāṇa* is restrained, there the mind is absorbed. –23.

दुग्धाम्बुवत्संमिलिताावुभौ तौ तुल्यक्रियौ मानसमारुतौ हि ।

यतो मरुत्तत्र मनः-प्रवृत्तिर् यतो मनस्तत्र मरुत्प्रवृत्तिः ॥२४॥

dugdhāmbuvatsaṃmilitāvubhau tau

tulyakriyau mānasamārutau hi ।

yato maruttatra manaḥpravṛttir

yato manastatra marutpravṛttiḥ ॥24॥

Mind and *prāṇa* are united together like milk and water; and both of them are equal in their activities. Where there is *prāṇa*, there is active presence of mind and where there is mind, there the *prāṇa* becomes active. –24.

तत्रैकनाशादपरस्य नाश एकप्रवृत्तेरपरप्रवृत्तिः ।

अध्वस्तयोश्चेन्द्रियवर्गवृत्तिः प्रध्वस्तयोर्मोक्षपदस्य सिद्धिः ॥२५॥

tatraikanāśādaparasya nāśa

ekapravṛtteraparapravṛttiḥ ।

adhvastayoścendriyavargavṛttiḥ

pradhvastayormokṣapadasya siddhiḥ ॥25॥

Therefore, if one is destroyed, another is (also) eradicated; if one is active, another also becomes active. If they are not destroyed, all the *indriyas* (the senses) are actively engaged in their respective jobs. If both of them are completely eradicated, *mokṣapada* (the state of liberation) is achieved. –25.

Mercurial Quality of Prāṇa and Mind

रसस्य मनसश्चैव चञ्चलत्वं स्वभावतः ।

रसो बद्धो मनो बद्धं किं न सिद्ध्यति भूतले ॥२६॥

rasasya manasaścaiva cañcalatvaṃ svabhāvataḥ ।

raso baddho mano baddhaṃ kiṃ na siddhyati bhūtale ॥26॥

Mercury and mind are unsteady by nature. By making mercury and mind stable, what cannot be accomplished on this earth? –26.

मूर्च्छितो हरते व्याधीन्मृतो जीवयति स्वयम् ।

बद्धः खेचरतां धत्ते रसो वायुश्च पार्वति ॥२७॥

mūrcchito harate vyādhīnmṛto jīvayati svayam ।

baddhaḥ khecaratāṃ dhatte raso vāyuśca pārvati ॥27॥

O *Pārvati*! When mercury and *prāṇa* are made stable, all diseases are eradicated; what is dead comes to life by itself. When they are captured, one moves in space. –27.

Pure State Depends on Stable Bindu

मनः स्थैर्यं स्थिरो वायुस्ततो बिन्दुः स्थिरो भवेत् ।

बिन्दुस्थैर्यात्सदा सत्त्वं पिण्डस्थैर्यं प्रजायते ॥२८॥

manaḥ sthairya sthiro vāyustato binduḥ sthiro bhavet ।

bindusthairyātsadā sattvaṃ piṇḍasthairyaṃ prajāyate ॥29॥

When the mind is steady, the *prāṇa* is also stable, and then the *bindu* (seminal।ovarian fluid) becomes stable. By the steadiness of the *bindu*, there results a *sāttvic* (pure) state which produces stillness in the body. –28.

Mind – the Master of Senses

इन्द्रियाणां मनो नाथो मनोनाथस्तु मारुतः ।

मारुतस्य लयो नाथः स लयो नादमाश्रितः ॥२९॥

indriyāṇāṃ mano nātho manonāthastu mārutaḥ ।

mārutasya layo nāthaḥ sa layo nādamāśritaḥ ॥29॥

Mind is the master of the senses and the *prāṇa* is the master of the mind. *Laya* (the absorption) is the lord of the *prāṇa*, and that *laya* depends on *nāda* (the mystical inner sound). –29.

Mokṣa – the Absorption of the Mind

सोऽयमेवास्तु मोक्षाख्यो मास्तु वापि मतान्तरे ।

मनःप्राणलये कश्चिदानन्दः सम्प्रवर्तते ॥३०॥

so'yamevāstu mokṣākhyo māstu vāpi matāntare ।

manaḥprāṇalaye kaścidānandaḥ sampravartate ॥30॥

This very absorption of the mind is called *mokṣa* (liberation), but others may say that it is not so. However, when the mind and the *prāṇa* are absorbed, unutterable joy is experienced. –30.

प्रनष्टश्वासनिश्वासः प्रध्वस्तविषयग्रहः ।

निश्चेष्टो निर्विकारश्च लयो जयति योगिनाम् ॥३१॥

prāṇaṣṭaśvāsaniśvāsaḥ pradhvastaviṣayagrahaḥ ।

niśceṣṭo nirvikāraśca layo jayati yoginām ॥31॥

When inhalation and exhalation are suspended, when the enjoyments of senses are annihilated and when there is an effortless and a changeless state of mind, then the yogī attains perfection in *laya* (absorption). –31.

Eradication of Desires Results in Laya

उच्छिन्नसर्वसङ्कल्पो निःशेषाशेषचेष्टितः ।

स्वावगम्यो लयः कोऽपि जायते वागगोचरः ॥३२॥

uccinnasarvasaṅkalpo niḥśeṣāśeṣaceṣṭitaḥ ।

svāvagamyo layaḥ ko'pi jāyate vāgagocaraḥ ॥32॥

When all the desires are eradicated and all the mental and physical activities are entirely stopped without any effort, the state of *laya* occurs which is only known by self-experience, and which is beyond the realm of words. –32.

यत्र दृष्टिर्लयस्तत्र भूतेन्द्रियसनातनी ।

सा शक्तिर्जीवभूतानां द्वे अलक्ष्ये लयं गते ॥३३॥

yatra dṛṣṭirlayastatra bhūtendriyasanātanī ।

sā śaktirjīvabhūtānāṃ dve alakṣye layaṃ gate ॥33॥

Where *dṛṣṭi* (the mental perception) is directed, there (in the Supreme) occurs absorption. That (i.e. *avidyā*) in which eternally exist *bhūtas* (the five elements) and *indriyas* (the five organs of senses and five organs of action), and that *śakti* (the Force) which is in all living beings, both are dissolved in *Alakṣya* (the Imperceptible i.e. Ultimate *Brahman*). –33.

The State of Laya

लयो लय इति प्राहुः कीदृशं लयलक्षणम् ।

अपुनर्वासनोत्थानाल्लयो विषयविस्मृतिः ॥३४॥

layo laya iti prāhuḥ kīdṛśaṃ layalakṣaṇam ।

apunarvāsanotthānāllayo viṣayavismṛtiḥ ॥34॥

People say "*laya, laya*", but what type of nature does *laya* have? *Laya* is simply non-recurrence of (previous) *vāsanas* (desires) and non-recalling of the sense objects. – 34.

Practice of Śāmbhavī Mudrā

अथ शाम्भवी ।

atha śāmbhavī ।

Now *śāmbhavī mudrā* is described.

वेदशास्त्रपुराणानि सामान्यगणिका इव ।

एकैव शाम्भवी मुद्रा गुप्ता कुलवधूरिव ॥३५॥

vedaśāstrapurāṇāni sāmānyagaṇikā iva ।

ekaiva śāmbhavī mudrā guptā kulavadhūriva ॥35॥

The *Vedas*, *Śāstras* and *Purāṇas* are like common public women. But *śāmbhavī mudrā* (concentration on the eye-brow center) alone is secret like a virtuous woman of a noble family. –35.

Śāmbhavī withdraws the Mind and Prāṇa

अन्तर्लक्ष्यं बहिर्दृष्टिर्निमेषोन्मेषवर्जिता ।

एषा सा शाम्भवी मुद्रा वेदशास्त्रेषु गोपिता ॥३६॥

antarlakṣyaṃ bahirdṛṣṭirnimeṣonmeṣavarjitā ।

eṣā sā śāmbhavī mudrā vedaśāstreṣu gopitā ॥36॥

Fixing the mind internally and keeping the eyes directed toward some external objects without blinking, is called *śāmbhavī mudrā*. It is kept secret in all the *Vedas* and *Śāstras*. –36.

अन्तर्लक्ष्यविलीनचित्तपवनो योगी यदा वर्तते

दृष्ट्या निश्चलतारया बहिरधः पश्यन्नपश्यन्नपि ।

मुद्रेयं खलु शाम्भवी भवति सा लब्धा प्रसादाद्गुरोः

शून्याशून्यविलक्षणं स्फुरति तत्तत्त्वं पदं शाम्भवम् ॥३७॥

antarlakṣyavilīnacittapavano yogī yadā vartate

dṛṣṭyā niścalatārayā bahiradhaḥ paśyannapaśyannapi ।

mudreyaṃ khalu śāmbhavī bhavati sā labdhā prasādādguroḥ

śūnyāśūnyavilakṣaṇaṃ sphurati tattattvaṃ padaṃ śāmbhavam ॥ 37॥

If the yogī remains with the mind and *prāṇa* absorbed in the internal object, gazing steadily with motionless pupils, and sees nothing while looking outside or down, this is indeed called *śāmbhavī mudrā*. When it is received by the grace of the guru, a wonderful sign of *śūnya* (the void) or *aśūnya* (non-void) is manifested within which is the supreme state and reality of *Śambhu*. –37.

श्रीशाम्भव्याश्च खेचर्या अवस्थाधामभेदतः ।

भवेच्चित्तलयानन्दः शून्ये चित्सुखरूपिणि ॥३८॥

śrīśāmbhavyāśca khecaryā avasthādhāmabhedataḥ ।

bhaveccittalayānandaḥ śūnye citsukharūpiṇi ॥38॥

Śāmbhavī and *khecarī* are two different states because of their seats or place of concentration, but both bring about absorption of mind in bliss and void, which is the form of supreme ecstatic state of consciousness. –38.

Practice of Unmanī

अथ उन्मनी ।

Atha unmani ।

Now *unmanī* is described.

तारे ज्योतिषि संयोज्य किंचिदुन्नमयेद्भ्रुवौ ।

पूर्वयोगं मनो युञ्जन्नुन्मनीकारकः क्षणात् ॥३९॥

tāre jyotiṣi saṃyojya kiñcidunnamayed bhruvau ।

pūrvayogaṃ mano yuñjannunmanīkārakaḥ kṣaṇāt ॥39॥

The pupils (of the eyes) should be directed towards the light by raising the eyebrows a little upward, and the mind should be joined in accordance with previously described yoga (*śāmbhavī mudrā*). This brings about the state of *unmanī* right away. –39.

Intricacy of Āgamas and Nigamas

केचिदागमजालेन केचिन्निगमसङ्कुलैः ।

केचित्तर्केण मुह्यन्ति नैव जानन्ति तारकम् ॥४०॥

kecidāgamajālena kecinnigamasaṅkulaiḥ ।

kecittarkeṇa muhyanti naiva jānanti tārakam ॥40॥

Some are confused by the intricacy of *Āgamas* (the *Śāstras* and *Tantras*), some are confused by the *Nigamas* (the *vedic* karmas - rituals and rites) and others are bewildered by logic, but they do not know what liberates them. –40.

Concentration on the Tip of the Nose

अर्धोन्मीलितलोचनः स्थिरमना नासाग्रदत्तेक्षणश्

चन्द्रार्कावपि लीनतामुपनयन्निस्पन्दभावेन यः ।

ज्योतीरुपमशेषबीजमखिलं देदीप्यमानं परं तत्त्वं

तत्पदमेति वस्तु परमं वाच्यं किमत्राधिकम् ॥४१॥

ardhonmīlitalocanaḥ sthiramanā nāsāgradattekṣaṇaś

candrārkāvapi līnatāmupanayannispandabhāvena yaḥ ।

jyotīrūpamaśeṣabījamakhilaṃ dedīpyamānaṃ paraṃ tattvaṃ

tatpadameti vastu paramaṃ vācyaṃ kimatrādhikam ॥41॥

With a steady mind and half closed eyes, fixed on the tip of the nose, suspending the *iḍā* and *piṅgalā* without blinking (or without any other physical movements), the yogī sees the form of *Jyoti* (light) which is endless, the source of all, radiant, and ultimate truth, and which is the supreme object to ever be attained. What more could be said? –41.

Right Time for Meditation Practice

दिवा न पूजयेल्लिङ्गं रात्रौ चैव न पूजयेत् ।

सर्वदा पूजयेल्लिङ्गं दिवारात्रिनिरोधतः ॥४२॥

divā na pūjayelliṅgaṃ rātrau caiva na pūjayet ।

sarvadā pūjayelliṅgaṃ divārātrinirodhataḥ ॥42॥

One should not worship (meditate upon) the *Liṅga* (the *Ātman*) in the day (when *prāṇa* is flowing through *sūrya* or *piṅgalā*) or at night (when *prāṇa* is flowing through the *candra* or *iḍā*). Always worship the *Liṅga* after restraining the day and night. –42.

Accomplishment of Khecarī Mudrā

अथ खेचरी ।

सव्यदक्षिणनाडीस्थो मध्ये चरति मारुतः ।

तिष्ठते खेचरी मुद्रा तस्मिन्स्थाने न संशयः ॥४३॥

atha khecarī ।

Now *khecarī* is described.

savyadakṣiṇanāḍīstho madhye carati mārutaḥ ।

tiṣṭhate khecarī mudrā tasminsthāne na saṃśayaḥ ॥43॥

When the *prāṇa* moves freely in the right and left *nāḍīs*, it naturally flows in the middle of the eyebrows (the *suṣumṇā*). In that spot (of the eyebrow center) *khecarī mudrā* is accomplished. There is no doubt about it. –43.

इडापिङ्गलयोर्मध्ये शून्यं चैवानिलं ग्रसेत् ।

तिष्ठते खेचरी मुद्रा तत्र सत्यं पुनः पुनः ॥४४॥

iḍāpiṅgalayormadhye śūnyaṃ caivānilaṃ graset ।

tiṣṭhate khecarī mudrā tatra satyaṃ punaḥ punaḥ ॥44॥

If the *prāṇa* is swallowed up (made motionless) in *śūnya* (the *suṣumṇā*) between the *iḍā* and *piṅgalā*, then *khecarī mudrā* becomes truly established there. –44.

सूर्याचन्द्रमसोर्मध्ये निरालम्बान्तरे पुनः ।

संस्थिता व्योमचक्रे या सा मुद्रा नाम खेचरी ॥४५॥

sūryācandramasormadhye nirālambāntare punaḥ ।

saṃsthitā vyomacakre yā sā mudrā nāma khecarī ॥45॥

The name of that *mudrā* is *khecarī* which is performed in the unsupported space of *vyoma cakra* (the center of ether or void) located between the sun (*iḍā*) and the moon (*piṅgalā*). –45.

सोमाद्यत्रोदिता धारा साक्षात्सा शिववल्लभा ।

पूरयेदतुलां दिव्यां सुषुम्णां पश्चिमे मुखे ॥४६॥

somādyatroditā dhārā sākṣāt sā śivavallabhā ।

pūrayedatulāṃ divyāṃ suṣumṇāṃ paścime mukhe ॥46॥

The *khecarī mudrā* that causes the stream of nectar to flow from the moon is beloved of *Śiva*. The divine *suṣumṇā*, unparalleled (in greatness), should be closed by the tongue turned upward and drawn back. –46.

Khecarī Mudrā leads to Unmanī

पुरस्ताच्चैव पूर्येत निश्चिता खेचरी भवेत् ।

अभ्यस्ता खेचरी मुद्राप्युन्मनी सम्प्रजायते ॥४७॥

purastāccaiva pūryeta niścitā khecarī bhavet ।

abhyastā khecarī mudrāpyunmanī samprajāyate ॥47॥

The *suṣumṇā* being filled from the front (at the rear of the upper palate) surely becomes *khecarī*. The constant practice of *khecarī mudrā* leads to the state of *unmanī*. –47.

भ्रुवोर्मध्ये शिवस्थानं मनस्तत्र विलीयते ।

ज्ञातव्यं तत्पदं तुर्यं तत्र कालो न विद्यते ॥४८॥

bhruvormadhye śivasthānaṃ manastatra vilīyate ।

jñātavyaṃ tatpadaṃ turyaṃ tatra kālo na vidyate ॥48॥

The seat of *Śiva* is between the eyebrows, and the mind is absorbed there. That state is known as *turīya avasthā* (the fourth state of consciousness, in which a union with *Brahma* takes is occurred), and death does not exist there. –48.

Yoga Nidrā through Khecarī

अभ्यसेत्खेचरीं तावद्यावत्स्याद्योगनिद्रितः ।

सम्प्राप्तयोगनिद्रस्य कालो नास्ति कदाचन ॥४९॥

abhyaset khecarīṃ tāvadyāvatsyādyoganidritaḥ ।

samprāptayoganidrasya kālo nāsti kadācana ॥49॥

One should practice *khecarī mudrā* until he gets into *yoga nidrā* (psychic sleep). He who has attained *yoga nidrā*, time does not exist for him. –49.

निरालम्बं मनः कृत्वा न किंचिदपि चिन्तयेत् ।

सबाह्याभ्यन्तरं व्योम्नि घटवत्तिष्ठति ध्रुवम् ॥५०॥

nirālambaṃ manaḥ kṛtvā na kiñcidāpi cintayet ।

sabāhyābhyantare vyomni ghaṭavattiṣṭhati dhruvam ॥50॥

Having made the mind unsupported, one should not think of anything at all. Then indeed he remains like a pot filled inside and outside with space. –50.

बाह्यवायुर्यथा लीनस्तथा मध्यो न संशयः ।

स्वस्थाने स्थिरतामेति पवनो मनसा सह ॥५१॥

bāhyavāyuryathā līnastathā madhyo na saṃśayaḥ ।

svasthāne sthiratāmeti pavano manasā saha ॥51॥

When the external *vāyu* is suspended, similarly the middle one (i.e. the *Śakti* in the *suṣumṇā*) is also suspended. There is no doubt that the *prāṇa*, along with the mind, will become steady in their place (i.e. in the *brahmarandhra*). –51.

एवमभ्यस्यतस्तस्य वायुमार्गे दिवानिशम् ।

अभ्यासाज्जीर्यते वायुर्मनस्तत्रैव लीयते ॥५२॥

evamabhyasyatastasya vāyumārge divāniśam ।

abhyāsājjīryate vāyurmanastatraiva līyate ॥52॥

By practicing thus with the breath in the path of *prāṇa* (the *suṣumṇā*) day and night, wherever the *prāṇa* is absorbed through practice, there the mind is dissolved. –52.

अमृतैः प्लावयेद्देहमापादतलमस्तकम् ।

सिद्ध्यत्येव महाकायो महाबलपराक्रमः ॥५३॥

amṛtaiḥ plāvayeddehamāpādatalamastakam ।

siddhyatyeva mahākāyo mahābalaparākramaḥ ॥53॥

The whole body from the head to the sole of the feet should be saturated with the flow of nectar. Thus, one attains a superior body, great strength and heroism. –53.

शक्तिमध्ये मनः कृत्वा शक्तिं मानसमध्यगाम् ।

मनसा मन आलोक्य धारयेत्परमं पदम् ॥५४॥

śaktimadhye manaḥ kṛtvā śaktiṃ mānasamadhyagām ।

manasā mana ālokya dhārayetparamaṃ padam ॥54॥

Having placed the mind in the *Śakti* (*Kuṇḍalinī*) and held the *Śakti* in the center of the mind, observe the mind with the mind and concentrate on *parama pada* (the supreme state - the object of concentration). –54.

खमध्ये कुरु चात्मानमात्ममध्ये च खं कुरु ।

सर्वं च खमयं कृत्वा न किंचिदपि चिन्तयेत् ॥५५॥

khamadhye kuru cātmānamātmamadhye ca khaṃ kuru ।

sarvaṃ ca khamayaṃ kṛtvā na kiñcidāpi cintayet ॥55॥

Place the *Ātmā* (Self) in the middle of *Ākāśa* (the *Brahman*) and keep the *Ākāśa* in the center of the *Ātmā*. Having pervaded everything with *Ākāśa* (i.e. having observed everything full of *Brahman*), one should not think of anything else. –55.

अन्तः शून्यो बहिः शून्यः शून्यः कुम्भ इवाम्बरे ।

अन्तः पूर्णो बहिः पूर्णः पूर्णः कुम्भ इवार्णवे ॥५६॥

antaḥ śūnyo bahiḥ śūnyaḥ śūnyaḥ kumbha ivāmbare ।

antaḥ pūrṇo bahiḥ pūrṇaḥ pūrṇaḥ kumbha ivārṇave ॥56॥

The yogī (in *samādhi* i.e. in deep meditation) should become void inside and outside, like a pot in space and full inside and outside like a jar in the ocean. –56.

बाह्यचिन्ता न कर्तव्या तथैवान्तरचिन्तनम् ।

सर्वचिन्तां परित्यज्य न किंचिदपि चिन्तयेत् ॥५७॥

bāhyacintā na kartavyā tathaivāntaracintanam ।

sarvacintāṃ parityajya na kiñcidāpi cintayet ॥57॥

He should have neither external (objective) thoughts nor internal (subjective) ones. Giving up all kinds of thoughts (both internal and external), he should think of nothing else. –57.

Thoughts Create the Universe

सङ्कल्पमात्रकलनैव जगत्समग्रं

सङ्कल्पमात्रकलनैव मनोविलासः ।

सङ्कल्पमात्रमतिमुत्सृज निर्विकल्पम्

आश्रित्य निश्चयमवाप्नुहि राम शान्तिम् ॥५८॥

saṅkalpamātrakalanaiva jagatsamagraṃ

saṅkalpamātrakalanaiva manovilāsaḥ ।

saṅkalpamātramatimutsṛja nirvikalpam

āśritya niścayamavāpnuhi rāma śāntim ॥

The whole universe is only created by thoughts. The play of the mind is only fabricated by thoughts. O *Rāma*! Having abandoned all creations of thought and taking shelter upon that which has no alternative, definitely attain everlasting peace. –58.

कर्पूरमनले यद्वत्सैन्धवं सलिले यथा ।

तथा सन्धीयमानं च मनस्तत्त्वे विलीयते ॥५९॥

karpūramanale yadvatsaindhavaṃ salile yathā ।

tathā sandhīyamānaṃ ca manastattve vilīyate ॥59॥

As camphor disappears in fire and salt in water, so the mind united with the *Ātmā*, is dissolved in the *Tattva* (the Truth or *Brahman*). –59.

ज्ञेयं सर्वं प्रतीतं च ज्ञानं च मन उच्यते ।

ज्ञानं ज्ञेयं समं नष्टं नान्यः पन्था द्वितीयकः ॥६०॥

jñeyaṃ sarvaṃ pratītaṃ ca jñānaṃ ca mana ucyate ।

jñānaṃ jñeyaṃ samaṃ naṣṭaṃ nānyaḥ panthā dvitīyakaḥ ॥60॥

All that is seen and experienced is called *jñeya* (the known) and the faculty of *jñāna* (knowledge) is called the mind. When the known and the knowledge are entirely destroyed, then there is no dual or second path. –60.

Duality Dissolves in Unmanī State

मनोदृश्यमिदं सर्वं यत्किंचित्सचराचरम् ।

मनसो ह्युन्मनीभावाद्द्वैतं नैवोलभ्यते ॥६१॥

manodṛśyamidāṃ sarvaṃ yatkiñcitsacarācaram ।

manaso hyunmanībhāvāddvaitaṃ naivopalabhyate ॥61॥

All which is animate or inanimate in this universe are images of the mind. When the mind attains the state of *unmanī*, there is no duality (i.e. it does not exist) –61.

ज्ञेयवस्तुपरित्यागाद्विलयं याति मानसम् ।

मनसो विलये जाते कैवल्यमवशिष्यते ॥६२॥

jñeyavastu parityāgādvilayaṃ yāti mānasam ।

manaso vilaye jāte kaivalyamavaśiṣyate ॥62॥

By abandoning the known objects, the mind goes into dissolution. When the mind is dissolved, then there remains *Kaivalya* (i.e. the absolute state) alone. –62.

एवं नानाविधोपायाः सम्यक्स्वानुभवान्विताः ।

समाधिमार्गाः कथिताः पूर्वाचार्यैर्महात्मभिः ॥६३॥

evaṃ nānāvidhopāyāḥ samyaksvānubhavānvitāḥ ।

samādhimārgāḥ kathitāḥ pūrvācāryairmahātmabhiḥ ॥63॥

In this way, there are various methods and paths that lead to *samādhi* told by those great ancient masters depending on their individual experiences. –63.

सुषुम्णायै कुण्डलिन्यै सुधायै चन्द्रजन्मने ।

मनोन्मन्यै नमस्तुभ्यं महाशक्त्यै चिदात्मने ॥६४॥

suṣumṇāyai kuṇḍalinyai sudhāyai candrājanmane ।

manonmanyai namastubhyaṃ mahāśaktyai cidātmane ॥64॥

Salutation to the *suṣumṇā*, to the *Kuṇḍalinī*, to the nectar generated from the moon, to the *manonmanī* (mind without mind or a mindless state) and to *Mahā Śakti* (the Great Power) in the form of *Cidātmā* (the Intelligent Spirit). –64.

Practice of Nāda as Told by Gorakṣanātha

अशक्यतत्त्वबोधानां मूढानामपि संमतम् ।

प्रोक्तं गोरक्षनाथेन नादोपासनमुच्यते ॥६५॥

aśakyatattvabodhānāṃ mūḍhānāmapi saṃmatam ।

proktaṃ gorakṣanāthena nādopāsanamucyate ॥65॥

I am going to describe now the practice of *nāda* (the inner mystical sound) as told by *Gorakṣanātha* which is accepted even by those ignorant who are unable to understand and realize the truth. –65.

Nāda Anusandhāna – A Way to Attain Laya

श्रीआदिनाथेन सपादकोटिलयप्रकाराः कथिता जयन्ति ।

नादानुसन्धानकमेकमेव मन्यामहे मुख्यतमं लयानाम् ॥६६॥

śrīādināthena sapādakoṭi-

layaprakārāḥ kathitā jayanti ।

nādānusandhānakamekameva

manyāmahe mukhyatamaṃ layānām ॥66॥

There are one and quarter crore (1,25,00,000) ways to attain *laya* told by *Śrī Ādinātha* (i.e. Lord *Śiva*), but of these, we think the one and only *nāda anusandhāna* (the technique of exploring the inner mystical sound) is the chief one. –66.

मुक्तासने स्थितो योगी मुद्रां सन्धाय शाम्भवीम् ।

शृणुयाद्दक्षिणे कर्णे नादमन्तास्थमेकधीः ॥६७॥

muktāsane sthito yogī mudrāṃ sandhāya śāmbhavīm ।

śṛṇuyāddakṣiṇe karṇe nādamantāsthamekadhīḥ ॥67॥

The yogī having seated in *muktāsana* should assume the *śāmbhavī mudrā* and listen to the sounds of internal *nāda* in the right ear with a concentrated mind. –67.

श्रवणपुटनयनयुगल घ्राणमुखानां निरोधनं कार्यम् ।

शुद्धसुषुम्णासरणौ स्फुटममलः श्रूयते नादः ॥६८॥

śravaṇapuṭanayanayugala

ghrāṇamukhānāṃ nirodhanaṃ kāryam ।

śuddhasuṣumṇāsaraṇau

sphuṭamamalaḥ śrūyate nādaḥ ॥68॥

Closing the ears, eyes, nose and mouth, a clear distinct sound of *nāda* is heard in the passage of the *suṣumṇā*, free from all impurities. –68.

आरम्भश्च घटश्चैव तथा परिचयोऽपि च ।

निष्पत्तिः सर्वयोगेषु स्यादवस्थाचतुष्टयम् ॥६९॥

ārambhaśca ghaṭaścaiva tathā paricayo'pi ca ।

niṣpattiḥ sarvayogeṣu syādavasthācatuṣṭayam ॥69॥

In all the yogic practices there are four stages: *ārambha* (preliminary), *ghaṭa* (literally, a vessel or jar), *paricaya* (knowing) and *nispatti* (consummation). –69.

Ārambha Avasthā – Beginning Stage

अथ आरम्भावस्था ।

ब्रह्मग्रन्थेर्भवेद्भेदो ह्यानन्दः शून्यसम्भवः ।

विचित्रः क्वणको देहेऽनाहतः श्रूयते ध्वनिः ॥७०॥

atha ārambhāvasthā ।

Now the state of *ārambha* is described.

brahmagrantherbhavedbhedo hyānandaḥ śūnyasambhavaḥ ।

vicitraḥ kvaṇako dehe'nāhataḥ śrūyate dhvaniḥ ॥70॥

When *Brahma granthi* (the knot of *Brahma*) is pierced, there is the feeling of bliss arising from *śūnya* (the void). Various wonderful tinkling sounds and the unstruck sound from the *anāhata cakra* (heart center) are heard within the body. –70.

दिव्यदेहश्च तेजस्वी दिव्यगन्धस्त्वरोगवान् ।

सम्पूर्णहृदयः शून्य आरम्भे योगवान्भवेत् ॥७१॥

divyadehaśca tejasvī divyagandhastvarogavān ।

sampūrṇahṛdayaḥ śūnya ārambhe yogavānbhavet ॥71॥

In the stage of *ārambha*, the body of the yogī becomes divine, radiant and free of disease, with a divine smell. He experiences fullness of heart and void within. –71.

Ghaṭa Avasthā – Vessel Stage

अथ घटावस्था ।

द्वितीयायां घटीकृत्य वायुर्भवति मध्यगः ।

दृढासनो भवेद्योगी ज्ञानी देवसमस्तदा ॥७२॥

atha ghaṭāvasthā ।

Now the stage of *ghaṭa* is described.

dvitīyāyāṃ ghaṭīkṛtya vāyurbhavati madhyagaḥ ।

dṛḍhāsano bhavedyogī jñānī devasamastadā ॥72॥

When *ghaṭa* is attained in the second stage, the *prāṇa* goes into the middle path (*suṣumṇā*). Then the yogī becomes steady in his posture, wise and equal to *devas* (the gods). –72.

विष्णुग्रन्थेस्ततो भेदात्परमानन्दसूचकः ।

अतिशून्ये विमर्दश्च भेरीशब्दस्तदा भवेत् ॥७३॥

viṣṇugranthestato bhedātparamānandasūcakaḥ ।

atiśūnye vimardaśca bherīśabdastadā bhavet ॥73॥

When the *Viṣṇu granthi* is pierced, it is the sign of *Paramānanda* (the Supreme Bliss). Then the pounding sound of the kettledrum is heard from the great void. –73.

Parichaya Avasthā – Perception Stage

अथ परिचयावस्था ।

तृतीयायां तु विज्ञेयो विहायो मर्दलध्वनिः ।

महाशून्यं तदा याति सर्वसिद्धिसमाश्रयम् ॥७४॥

atha paricayāvasthā ।

Now the stage of *paricaya* is described.

tṛtīyāyāṃ tu vijñeyo vihāyomardaladhvaniḥ ।

mahāśūnyaṃ tadā yāti sarvasiddhisamāśrayam ॥74॥

In the third stage, the sound of *mardala* (a kind of drum) is heard in the space between the eyebrows and then the *prāṇa* goes to *mahāśūnya* (the great void) which is the shelter of all *siddhis*. –74.

चित्तानन्दं तदा जित्वा सहजानन्दसम्भवः ।

दोषदुःखजराव्याधिक्षुधानिद्राविवर्जितः ॥७५॥

cittānandaṃ tadā jitvā sahajānandasambhavaḥ ।

doṣaduḥkhajarāvyādhikṣudhānidrāvivarjitaḥ ॥75॥

Having conquered *cittānanda* (the blissful state of mind), he experiences *sahajānanda* (the natural state of bliss arising from self-realization). Then he becomes free from faults, pain, old age, disease, hunger and sleep. –75.

Niṣpatti Avasthā – Final Stage

अथ निष्पत्ति अवस्था ।

रुद्रग्रन्थिं यदा भित्त्वा शर्वपीठगतोऽनिलः ।

निष्पत्तौ वैणवः शब्दः क्वणद्वीणाक्वणो भवेत् ॥७६॥

atha niṣpatti avasthā ।

Now the stage of *niṣpatti* is described.

rudragranthiṃ yadā bhittvā śarvapīṭhagato'nilaḥ ।

niṣpattau vaiṇavaḥ śabdaḥ kvaṇadvīṇākvaṇo bhavet ॥76॥

When the *Rudra granthi* is pierced, the *prāṇa* enters into the seat of Lord *Śiva*. Then in the stage of *nispatti* the tinkling sounds of the flute resonating like *vīṇā* (a large lute) are heard. –76.

एकीभूतं तदा चित्तं राजयोगाभिधानकम् ।

सृष्टिसंहारकर्तासौ योगीश्वरसमो भवेत् ॥७७॥

ekībhūtaṃ tadā cittaṃ rājayogābhidhānakam ।

sṛṣṭisaṃhārakartāsau yogīśvarasamo bhavet ॥77॥

When the mind becomes one (with the object of concentration), it is called *Rāja Yoga*. The yogī, being the creator and destroyer of the universe, becomes equal to *Isvara*. –77.

अस्तु वा मास्तु वा मुक्तिरत्रैवाखण्डितं सुखम् ।

लयोद्भवमिदं सौख्यं राजयोगादवाप्यते ॥७८॥

astu vā māstu vā muktiratraivākhaṇḍitaṃ sukham ।

layodbhavamidāṃ saukhyaṃ rājayogādavāpyate ॥78॥

Whether there is *mukti* (liberation) or not, here he attains uninterrupted bliss. The bliss arising from *laya* is achieved through (the practice of) *Rāja Yoga*. –78.

Haṭha Yoga without Rāja Yoga is Fruitless

राजयोगमजानन्तः केवलं हठकर्मिणः ।

एतानभ्यासिनो मन्ये प्रयासफलवर्जितान् ॥७९॥

rājayogamajānantaḥ kevalaṃ haṭhakarmiṇaḥ ।

etānabhyāsino manye prayāsaphalavarjitān ॥79॥

There are merely *Haṭha Yogīs* (*Haṭha Yoga* practitioners) without the knowledge of *Rāja Yoga*. I consider them to be simply practitioners who do not derive the fruits of their efforts. –79.

उन्मन्यवाप्तये शीघ्रं भ्रूध्यानं मम संमतम् ।
राजयोगपदं प्राप्तुं सुखोपायोऽल्पचेतसाम् ।
सद्यः प्रत्ययसन्धायी जायते नादजो लयः ॥८०॥

unmanyavāptaye śīghraṃ bhrūdhyānaṃ mama saṃmatam ।
rājayogapadaṃ prāptuṃ sukhopāyo'lpacetasām ।
sadyaḥ pratyayasandhāyī jāyate nādajo layaḥ ॥80॥

In my opinion, contemplation on the space between the eyebrows is best for attaining the *unmanī* state quickly. Even for people with less intellect, it is a comfortable method for attaining *rājayogapada* (the highest state of *Rāja Yoga*). The *laya* achieved through (the practice of) *nāda* gives immediate experience. –80.

Nādānusandhāna Leads to Samādhi

नादानुसन्धानसमाधिभाजां
योगीश्वराणां हृदि वर्धमानम् ।
आनन्दमेकं वचसामगम्यं
जानाति तं श्रीगुरुनाथ एकः ॥८१॥

nādānusandhānasamādhibhājāṃ
yogīśvarāṇāṃ hṛdi vardhamānam ।
ānandamekaṃ vacasāmagamyaṃ
jānāti taṃ śrīgurunātha ekaḥ ॥81॥

There is a huge augmentation of bliss in the hearts of the *Yogīśvaras* (lords of yogīs) who have attained success in *samādhi* by means of *nādānusandhāna* (the exploration of *nāda* or inner mystical sound) which is beyond all descriptions, and it is known by one *Śrī Gurunātha* (the Lord of the Gurus i.e. *Śiva*) alone. –81.

कर्णौ पिधाय हस्ताभ्यां यः शृणोति ध्वनिं मुनिः ।
तत्र चित्तं स्थिरीकुर्याद्यावत्स्थिरपदं व्रजेत् ॥८२॥

karṇau pidhāya hastābhyāṃ yaṃ śṛṇoti dhvaniṃ muniḥ ।

tatra cittaṃ sthirīkuryādyāvat sthirapadaṃ vrajet ॥82॥

Having closed the ears with the hands, the *muni* (sage or ascetic) should listen to the (inner) sounds and make his mind stable there until *sthirapada* (the state of complete steadiness of mind) is attained. –82.

अभ्यस्यमानो नादोऽयं बाह्यमावृणुते ध्वनिम् ।

पक्षाद्विक्षेपमखिलं जित्वा योगी सुखी भवेत् ॥८३॥

abhyāsyamāno nādo'yaṃ bāhyamāvṛṇute dhvanim ।

pakṣādvikṣepamakhilaṃ jitvā yogī sukhī bhavet ॥83॥

By the constant practice of this *nāda*, all the external sounds are diminished. Having conquered all the mental distractions within fifteen days, the yogī becomes happy. –83.

Types of Nādas Heard।Perceived

श्रूयते प्रथमाभ्यासे नादो नानाविधो महान् ।

ततोऽभ्यासे वर्धमाने श्रूयते सूक्ष्मसूक्ष्मकः ॥८४॥

śrūyate prathamābhyāse nādo nānāvidho mahān ।

tato'bhyāse vardhamāne śrūyate sūkṣmasūkṣmakaḥ ॥84॥

During the initial practice various great *nādas* are heard. But when the practice is prolonged, the subtler of the subtle sounds are heard. –84.

आदौ जलधिजीमूतभेरीझर्झरसम्भवाः ।

मध्ये मर्दलशङ्खोत्था घण्टाकाहलजास्तथा ॥८५॥

ādau jaladhijīmūtabherījharjharasambhavāḥ ।

madhye mardalaśaṅkhotthā ghaṇṭākāhalajāstathā ॥85॥

In the beginning, the sounds are similar to those of the ocean, then the clouds, kettledrum and *jharjhara* (a kind of drum - cymbal). In the middle the sounds resemble those of the *mardala* (a kind of drum), the conch, the bell and the *kāhala* (large drum used by the military). –85.

अन्ते तु किङ्किणीवंशवीणाभ्रमर निःस्वनाः ।

इति नानाविधा नादाः श्रूयन्ते देहमध्यगाः ॥८६॥

ante tu kiṅkiṇīvaṃśavīṇābhramara niḥsvanāḥ ।

iti nānāvidhā nādāḥ śrūyante dehamadhyagāḥ ॥86॥

In the end they resemble those of the tinkling bell, flute, *vīṇā* (the Indian lute) and humming of wild bees. Thus, these various kinds of *nādas* are heard from the middle of the body. –86.

महति श्रूयमाणेऽपि मेघभेर्यादिके ध्वनौ ।

तत्र सूक्ष्मात्सूक्ष्मतरं नादमेव परामृशेत् ॥८७॥

mahāti śrūyamāṇe'pi meghabheryādike dhvanau ।

tatra sūkṣmātsūkṣmataraṃ nādameva parāmṛśet ॥87॥

Even though the great sounds of clouds and kettledrums are heard, the practitioner should focus his mind on the subtlest of the subtle *nādas* there (within the body). –87.

घनमुत्सृज्य वा सूक्ष्मे सूक्ष्ममुत्सृज्य वा घने ।

रममाणमपि क्षिप्तं मनो नान्यत्र चालयेत् ॥८८॥

ghanamutsṛjya vā sūkṣme sūkṣmamutsṛjya vā ghane ।

ramamāṇamapi kṣiptaṃ mano nānyatra cālayet ॥88॥

Although the practitioner may be shifting his attention from loud to subtle sounds or from subtle to loud ones, fixing his mind on pleasing subtle sounds, he should not allow his mind to wander away. –88.

यत्र कुत्रापि वा नादे लगति प्रथमं मनः ।

तत्रैव सुस्थिरीभूय तेन सार्धं विलीयते ॥८९॥

yatra kutrāpi vā nāde lagati prathamaṃ manaḥ ।

tatraiva susthirībhūya tena sārdhaṃ vilīyate ॥89॥

Wherever the mind attaches itself to the *nāda* first, it becomes perfectly steady there and dissolves together with it. –89.

Mind Merges in Nāda

मकरन्दं पिबन्भृङ्गी गन्धं नापेक्षते यथा ।

नादासक्तं तथा चित्तं विषयान्नहि काङ्क्षते ॥१०॥

makarandaṃ pibanbhṛṅgo gandhaṃ nāpekṣate yathā ।

nādāsaktaṃ tathā cittaṃ viṣayānnahi kāṅkṣate ॥*90*॥

Just as a bee drinking the honey of the flowers does not care for the smell (of the flower), so the mind strongly attached to *nāda* does not desire for any objects of sensual enjoyment. –90.

मनोमत्तगजेन्द्रस्य विषयोद्यानचारिणः ।

समर्थोऽयं नियमने निनादनिशिताङ्कुशः ॥९१॥

manomattagajendrasya viṣayodyānacāriṇaḥ ।
samartho'yaṃ niyamane ninādaniśitāṅkuśaḥ ॥*91*॥

The sharp goad of *nāda* is fully capable of controlling the mind, which is like a furious elephant roaming in the garden of sensual enjoyment. –91.

Mind Stops Wandering in Nāda

बद्धं तु नादबन्धेन मनः सन्त्यक्तचापलम् ।

प्रयाति सुतरां स्थैर्यं छिन्नपक्षः खगो यथा ॥९२॥

baddhaṃ tu nādabandhena manaḥ santyaktacāpalam ।

prayāti sutarāṃ sthairyaṃ chinnapakṣaḥ khago yathā ॥*92*॥

When the mind is bound by the noose of the *nāda*, giving up its very wandering nature, it quickly comes to the state of steadiness, like a bird that has cut off its wings. –92.

सर्वचिन्तां परित्यज्य सावधानेन चेतसा ।

नाद एवानुसन्धेयो योगसाम्राज्यमिच्छता ॥९३॥

sarvacintāmparityajya sāvadhānena cetasā ।

nāda evānusandheyo yogasāmrājyamicchatā ॥*93*॥

Giving up all thoughts, the yogī, who is desirous of receiving the kingdom of yoga, should thus practice the exploration of *nāda* with a careful and alert mind. –93.

नादोऽन्तरङ्गसारङ्गबन्धने वागुरायते ।

अन्तरङ्गकुरङ्गस्य वधे व्याधायतेऽपि च ॥९४॥

nādo'ntaraṅgasāraṅgabandhane vāgurāyate ।

antaraṅgakuraṅgasya vadhe vyādhāyate'pi ca ॥94॥

Nāda is like the snare for entrapping the deer (mind) within. It is also like the hunter who kills the deer (mind) inside. –94.

अन्तरङ्गस्य यमिनो वाजिनः परिघायते ।

नादोपास्तिरतो नित्यमवधार्या हि योगिना ॥९५॥

antaraṅgasya yamino vājinaḥ parighāyate ।

nādopāstirato nityamavadhāryā hi yoginā ॥95॥

For a self-restrained yogī, *nāda* is like a bolt of a stable that locks a horse inside. Therefore, the yogī should constantly engage in the practice of concentrating upon *nāda* with a collected mind. –95.

बद्धं विमुक्तचाञ्चल्यं नादगन्धकजारणात् ।

मनःपारदमाप्नोति निरालम्बाख्यखेऽटनम् ॥९६॥

baddhaṃ vimuktacāñcalyaṃ nādagandhakajāraṇāt ।

manaḥ pāradamāpnoti nirālambākhyakhe'ṭanam ॥96॥

Just as liquid mercury is made solid by sulphur and has its unstable nature removed, so the mind is made steady by *nāda* and then it moves into the unsupported space of eternity called void. –96.

नादश्रवणतः क्षिप्रमन्तरङ्गभुजङ्गमम् ।

विस्मृतय सर्वमेकाग्रः कुत्रचिन्नहि धावति ॥९७॥

nādaśravaṇataḥ kṣipramantaraṅgabhujaṅgamaḥ ।

vismṛtaya sarvamekāgraḥ kutracinnahi dhāvati ॥97॥

By hearing the (music of) *nāda*, the mind is quickly fascinated like a serpent within. Having forgotten everything else, it remains concentrated, and does not run away anywhere. –97.

काष्ठे प्रवर्तितो वह्निः काष्ठेन सह शाम्यति ।

नादे प्रवर्तितं चित्तं नादेन सह लीयते ॥९८॥

kāṣṭhe pravartito vahniḥ kāṣṭhena saha śāmyati ।

nāde pravartitaṃ cittaṃ nādena saha līyate ॥98॥

The fire kindled in the firewood is extinguished together with the wood when it is burnt up. So the mind incited by the *nāda* is dissolved together with it. –98.

घण्टादिनादसक्तस्तब्धान्तःकरणहरिणस्य ।

प्रहरणमपि सुकरं शरसन्धानप्रवीणश्चेत् ॥९९॥

ghaṇṭādinādasaktastabdhāntaḥkaraṇahariṇasya ।

praharaṇamapi sukaraṃ śarasandhānapravīṇaścet ॥99॥

Just like a deer attracted by the sounds of bells, the *antaḥkaraṇa* (mind) absorbed in *nāda* becomes steady. Then it is very easy for an expert archer to kill it. –99.

The Supreme Object of Nāda

अनाहतस्य शब्दस्य ध्वनिर्य उपलभ्यते ।

ध्वनेरन्तर्गतं ज्ञेयं ज्ञेयस्यान्तर्गतं मनः ।

मनस्तत्र लयं याति तद्विष्णोः परमं पदम् ॥१००॥

anāhatasyaśabdasya dhvanirya upalabhyate ।

dhvanerantargataṃ jñeyaṃ jñeyasyāntargataṃ manaḥ ।

manastatra layaṃ yāti tadviṣṇoḥ paramaṃ padam ॥100॥

The unstruck resonance of *anāhata śabda* (the sound) becomes audible (to the practitioner) in which the supreme object (of knowledge) exists. The mind becomes one with that object of knowledge. That is *parampada* (the supreme state) of *Viṣṇu* (the All-pervading One) where the mind is dissolved. –100.

The Ultimate State is Soundless

तावदाकाशसङ्कल्पो यावच्छब्दः प्रवर्तते ।

निःशब्दं तत्परं ब्रह्म परमात्म इति गीयते ॥१०१॥

tāvadākāśasaṅkalpo yāvacchabdaḥ pravartate ।

niḥśabdaṃ tatparaṃ brahma paramātma iti gīyate ॥101॥

So long as the sound is heard, the concept of *ākāśa* (the ether or space) exists. The soundless is *Parama Brahma* (the Ultimate Reality) which is also called *Paramātmā* (the Supreme or Universal Self). –101.

All Forms of Nāda is Śakti, Formless is Eternal

यत्किंचिन्नादरूपेण श्रूयते शक्तिरेव सा ।

यस्तत्त्वान्तो निराकारः स एव परमेश्वरः ॥१०२॥

yatkiñcinnādarūpeṇa śrūyate śaktireva sā ।

yastattvānto nirākāraḥ sa eva parameśvaraḥ ॥102॥

Whatever is heard in the form of *nāda*, it is indeed *śakti*. That which is the final state of *tattvas* (the elements), *nirākāra* (the formless) is in fact *Parameśvara* (the Supreme Being।God). –102.

इति नादानुसन्धानम् ।

iti nādānusandhānam ।

Thus here ends *nādānusandhāna*.

Haṭha and Yoga for Rāja Yoga Alone

सर्वे हठलयोपाया राजयोगस्य सिद्धये ।

राजयोगसमारूढः पुरुषः कालवञ्चकः ॥१०३॥

sarve haṭhalayopāyā rājayogasya siddhaye ।

rājayogasamārūḍhaḥ puruṣaḥ kālavañcakaḥ ॥103॥

All the methods of *Haṭhayoga* and *Layayoga* practices are solely for the fulfillment of *Rāja Yoga*. One who has highly established in *Rāja Yoga* is the deceiver of *kāla* (death or time). –103.

A Detached Mind Attains Unmanī

तत्त्वं बीजं हठः क्षेत्रमौदासीन्यं जलं त्रिभिः ।

उन्मनी कल्पलतिका सद्य एव प्रवर्तते ॥१०४॥

tattvaṃ bījaṃ haṭhaḥ kṣetramaudāsīnyaṃ jalaṃ tribhiḥ ।

unmanī kalpalatikā sadya eva pravartate ॥104॥

Tattva (the mind) is the seed, *Haṭha Yoga* is the field and *udāsīna* (total detachment i.e. indifference towards worldly sense-objects) is water. By these three, the *kalpa latika* (literally, a heavenly creeper that gives whatever is desired), which is the state of *unmanī* (the state beyond mind) surely flourishes right away. – 104.

Nāda Practice Destroys All Sins

सदा नादानुसन्धानात्क्षीयन्ते पापसंचयाः ।

निरञ्जने विलीयेते निश्चितं चित्तमारुतौ ॥१०५॥

sadā nādānusandhānātkṣīyante pāpasañcayāḥ ।

nirañjane vilīyete niścitaṃ cittamārutau ॥105॥

Through the constant practice of the exploration of *nāda*, various accumulated heaps of sins are destroyed. The mind and the *prāṇa* both are certainly dissolved into *Nirañjana* (the pure consciousness which is free from all qualities।dualities). –105.

शङ्खदुन्धुभिनादं च न शृणोति कदाचन ।

काष्ठवज्जायते देह उन्मन्यावस्थया ध्रुवम् ॥१०६॥

śaṅkhadundhubhinādaṃ ca na śṛṇoti kadācana ।

kāṣṭhavajjāyate deha unmanyāvasthayā dhruvam ॥106॥

The body certainly becomes like a log of wood during *unmanī avasthā* (the state beyond mind). The yogī neither hears the loud sounds of *śaṅkha* (the conch) nor *dundubhi* (the large drum). –106.

A Yogī Liberates Himself While Living

सर्वावस्थाविनिर्मुक्तः सर्वचिन्ताविवर्जितः ।

मृतवत्तिष्ठते योगी स मुक्तो नात्र संशयः ॥१०७॥

sarvāvasthāvinirmuktaḥ sarvacintāvivarjitaḥ ।

mṛtavattiṣṭhate yogī sa mukto nātra saṃśayaḥ ॥107॥

The yogī who has reached beyond all states and is freed from all thoughts।memories, remains like one (who is) dead. There is no doubt that he is liberated while living. –107.

Nothing Affects a Yogī in Samādhi

खाद्यते न च कालेन बाध्यते न च कर्मणा ।

साध्यते न स केनापि योगी युक्तः समाधिना ॥१०८॥

khādyate na ca kālena bādhyate na ca karmaṇā ।

sādhyate na sa kenāpi yogī yuktaḥ samādhinā ॥108॥

The yogī who is absorbed in *samādhi* is not devoured by *kāla* (death।time). He is not bound by any karma (good or bad), nor can he be controlled by any means. –108.

No Sense Perception in Samādhi

न गन्धं न रसं रूपं न च स्पर्शं न निःस्वनम् ।

नात्मानं न परं वेत्ति योगी युक्तः समाधिना ॥१०९॥

na gandhaṃ na rasaṃ rūpaṃ na ca sparśaṃ na niḥsvanam ।

nātmānaṃ na paraṃ vetti yogī yuktaḥ samādhinā ॥109॥

A yogī engaged in *samādhi* knows neither smell, taste, form, touch nor sound. He knows neither himself nor others. –109.

Symptoms of a Liberated Yogī

चित्तं न सुप्तं नोजाग्रत्स्मृतिविस्मृतिवर्जितम् ।

न चास्तमेति नोदेति यस्यासौ मुक्त एव सः ॥११०॥

na suptaṃ nojāgratsmṛtivismṛtivarjitam ।

na cāstameti nodeti yasyāsau mukta eva saḥ ॥110॥

A yogī is indeed called liberated when his mind is neither asleep nor awake or when he is free from *smṛti* (memory) and *vismṛti* (forgetfulness) or when he is neither setting down (dead) nor rising up (living). –110.

न विजानाति शीतोष्णं न दुःखं न सुखं तथा ।

न मानं नोपमानं च योगी युक्तः समाधिना ॥१११॥

na vijānāti śītoṣṇaṃ na duḥkhaṃ na sukhaṃ tathā ।

na mānaṃ napamānaṃ ca yogī yuktaḥ samādhinā ॥111॥

The yogī absorbed in *samādhi* does not know।feel heat and cold, pain and pleasure and honor and dishonor. –111.

स्वस्थो जाग्रदवस्थायां सुप्तवद्योऽवतिष्ठते ।

निःश्वासोच्छ्वासहीनश्च निश्चितं मुक्त एव सः ॥११२॥

svastho jāgradavasthāyāṃ suptavadyo'vatiṣṭhate ।

niḥśvāsocchvāsahīnaśca niścitaṃ mukta eva saḥ ॥112॥

He who remains asleep in the waking state, who is without inhalation and exhalation, yet is in a healthy condition, is certainly liberated. –112.

अवध्यः सर्वशस्त्राणामशक्यः सर्वदेहिनाम् ।

अग्राह्यो मन्त्रयन्त्राणां योगी युक्तः समाधिना ॥११३॥

avadhyaḥ sarvaśastrāṇāmaśakyaḥ sarvadehinām ।

agrāhyo mantrayantrāṇāṃ yogī yuktaḥ samādhinā ॥113॥

A yogī in *samādhi* is invulnerable to all weapons; he is beyond the control of all beings and beyond the reach of all *mantras* (incantations, invocations and charms, etc.) and *yantras* (astrological diagrams). –113.

The Ultimate Purpose of Yoga

यावन्नैव प्रविशति चरन्मारुतो मध्यमार्गे

यावद्बिदुर्न भवति दृढः प्राणवातप्रबन्धात् ।

यावद्ध्याने सहजसदृशं जायते नैव तत्त्वं

तावज्ज्ञानं वदति तदिदं दम्भमिथ्याप्रलापः ॥११४॥

yāvanaiva praviśati caranmaruto madyamārge

yāvadvidurna bhavati dṛḍhaḥ prāṇavātaprabandhāt ।

yāvaddhyāne sahajasadṛśaṃ jāyate naiva tattvaṃ

tāvajjñānaṃ vadati tadidāṃ dambhamithyāpralāpaḥ ॥114॥

So long as the *prāṇa* does not flow in *madhyamarga* (literally, the middle passage i.e. *suṣumṇā*), so long as the *bindu* (seminal fluid) is not stabilized by restraining *prāṇa vāyu* (the vital energy or life force), so long as the mind does not naturally become of a similar nature to the object contemplated upon (the Ultimate *Brahman*) in meditation, then he who talks of spiritual knowledge and wisdom is a hypocrite and just does nonsense chatting in vain. –114.

इति हठयोगप्रदीपिकायां चतुर्थोपदेशः ।

iti haṭhayogapradīpikāyāṃ caturthopadeśaḥ ॥

Thus ends the Chapter Four of *Haṭha Yoga Pradīpikā.*

A KEY TO TRANSLITERATION

Vowels

अ आ इ ई उ ऊ ऋ ॠ

a ā i ī u ū ṛ ṝ

ऌ ॡ ए ऐ ओ औ अं अः

lṛ lṝ e ai o au aṃ aḥ

Consonants

क ख ग घ ङ - Gutturals:

ka kha ga gha ṅa

च छ ज झ ञ - Palatals:

ca cha ja jha ña

ट ठ ड ढ ण - Cerebrals:

ṭa ṭha ḍa ḍha ṇa

त थ द ध न - Dentals:

ta tha da dha na

प फ ब भ म - Labials:

pa pha ba bha ma

य र ल व - Semivowels:

ya ra la va

श ष स ह - Sibilants:

śa ṣa sa ha

क्ष त्र ज्ञ - Compound Letters:

kṣa tra jña

Aspirate: ह - ha, Anusvara: अं - aṃ

Visharga - aḥ - अः

Unpronounced अ - a - ऽ - ’, आ - ā - ऽऽ - ”

ALSO BY THIS AUTHOR

Yoga Kundalini Upanishad (in English)

Yoga Darshana Upanishad (in English)

Minor Yoga Upanishads (in English)

Hatha Yoga Pradipoka (in English)

Yogatattva Upanishad (in English)

Two Yoga Samhitas (in English)

Triyoga Upanishad (in English)

Gheranda Samhita (in English)

Goraksha Samhita (in English)

Surya Namskara (in Nepali)

Shiva Samhita (in English)

Shiva Samhita (in Nepali)

Durga Strotram (in Nepali)

Vagalamukhi Stotram (in Nepali)

Amogha Shivakavacham (in Nepali)

ABOUT THE AUTHOR

Swami Vishnuswaroop (Thakur Krishna Uprety), B. A. (Majored in English & Economics), received his Diploma in Yogic Studies (First Class) from Bihar Yoga Bharati, Munger, Bihar, India. He was formally trained under the direct guidance and supervision of Swami Niranjanananda Saraswati in the Guru Kula tradition of the Bihar School of Yoga. He was initiated into the lineage of Swami Satyananda Saraswati, the founder of Bihar School of Yoga and the direct disciple of Swami Sivananda Saraswati of Rishikesh. His guru gave his spiritual name 'Vishnuswaroop' while he was initiated into the sannyasa tradition.

Swami Vishnuswaroop is a Life Member of World Yoga Council, International Yoga Federation. Divine Yoga Institute has published his nine books on classical yoga, meditation and tantra. He is one of the few yoga practitioners registered with Nepal Health Professional Council established by The Government of Nepal. He has been teaching on the theory and practice of traditional yoga and the yogic way of life to Nepalese and foreign nationals for more than twenty-five years.

Swami Vishnuswaroop has designed a comprehensive yoga program called 'Yoga Passport' in order to give a broader theoretical and practical knowledge of yoga which includes various aspects of yogic practice. Many health professionals, yoga practitioners and people from various backgrounds of more than forty-seven countries from various parts of the world have gone through his yoga courses and programs. He currently works as the President of Divine Yoga Institute, Kathmandu, Nepal and travels abroad to provide yogic teaching and training.

ABOUT THE PUBLISHER

Divine Yoga Institute, which follows Satyananda Yoga tradition, offers a wide variety of group and individual courses in Yogic art and science. Classes at the Institute contribute to the development of a healthy body, a healthy mind, and healthy thought. Institute teachers help students achieve balanced, harmonious and integrated development of all the aspects of their personalities.

The goal of the Divine Yoga Institute is to promote a Yogic system of life with Yoga as a pathway to true, happy, and healthy living. Yogic training eventually prepares one for spiritual awakening, the supreme aim of human life. Keeping in view of this fact objective Divine Yoga Institute has published nine books on classical yoga, meditation and tantra authored and translated by Swami Vishnuswaroop.

Divine Yoga Institute has published his nine books on classical yoga, meditation and tantra. He is one of the few yoga practitioners registered with Nepal Health Professional Council established by The Government of Nepal. He has been teaching on the theory and practice of traditional yoga and the yogic way of life to Nepalese and foreign nationals for more than twenty-five years.

We have special yoga programs in the following areas: Yoga Passport program for comprehensive, intensive courses, Yogic Health and Wellness Management, Yogic Therapy for specific health problems, Shatkarma (Yogic Cleansing Practices), Yoga Teacher Training, Yoga Therapy Training and Yoga Philosophy.

Divine Yoga Institute was established in 1998 by a team of qualified Yoga professionals who received their academic degrees from Bihar Yoga Bharati (BYB) in the *Guru Kula* tradition of Bihar School of Yoga (BSY), Munger, India. BYB is the first Yoga Institute for advanced yogic studies of its kind in the world. Divine Yoga Institute follows the BSY/BYB method of teaching, founded by *Swami Satyananda Saraswati*, a direct disciple of *Swami Shivananda Saraswati* of Rishikesh. *Swami Satyananda* promoted the most profound and holistic aspects of Yoga, covering body, mind, emotions, intellect, spirit and karma. He was the first to widely popularize and spread the therapeutic effects of Yoga.

Made in United States
North Haven, CT
22 April 2022

18483785R00079